A
GREAT
HONOR

Alan Boyd

A GREAT HONOR

MY LIFE SHAPING 20TH CENTURY TRANSPORTATION

ALAN S. BOYD

Artisan Island Press

Portland, Maine

ISBN: 978-0-692-68296-8

MANUFACTURED IN THE UNITED STATES OF AMERICA

Design by Ray Rhamey

First Edition, June 2016

DEDICATION

To the loving memory of
Flavil Townsend Boyd,
without whom even this interesting life
would have been boring.

PROLOGUE

Surprise

By the spring of 1965, I had worked in Washington, DC, as a member, and then chairman, of the Civil Aeronautics Board for almost six years. I had found it interesting and rewarding, but I was ready for a new challenge. I informed the White House that they should find a replacement for me so that I could return to my law practice in Miami, Florida.

About a month later, I was having lunch at the Metropolitan Club two blocks from the White House when I was told there was a phone call for me. It was my friend Jim Jones, President Lyndon Johnson's appointments secretary. He said, "Alan, the president is having a press conference at one o'clock and he wants you to be here. Come over now."

I walked over immediately, entered Jim's office, and said, "What the hell is going on?"

"It's a secret. I can't tell you, Alan," Jim said. "But it's time to go." We left his office with two gentlemen who had been sitting in his anteroom and proceeded to the East Room of the White House, which was arranged for a press conference. There were three chairs in front for myself and the other two men, Wilbur Cohen and Lieutenant General "Bozo" McKee.

Soon President Johnson came in and said he had a few announcements to make. First and foremost, he was nominating his old friend Wilbur Cohen to become under secretary of health, education, and welfare. He praised Wilbur's virtues and experience in government. Then he talked of his admiration for General McKee and his accomplishments in the air force, and named him administrator of the Federal Aviation Agency. At this point I was completely mystified. I had thought I might be selected to become the next Federal Aviation administrator. With the nomination of General McKee to that role, however, I was puzzled about why I was here, to say the least.

With great interest, I heard President Johnson say, "I am very proud to nominate my good friend Alan Boyd to be under secretary of commerce for transportation. He knows more about transportation than anyone I know and has done a superb job as chairman of the Civil Aeronautics Board." He went on to extol my competence and skill while I sat there trying to catch my breath. It was true that I had a great knowledge of transportation, but I knew nothing of what the president had in mind for me that day. I couldn't very well stand up and say, "Excuse me, Mr. President, I'd like to think about it, talk to my wife, and then get back to you." That wouldn't be the only time LBJ would surprise me.

I

Preparing the Way

In July 1922, my father drove my mother the twenty-eight miles from Macclenny to Jacksonville, Florida, over a section of US Highway 90 that he was responsible for paving. In the early morning hours of July 20, I drew my first breath at Saint Luke's Hospital. A year and a day later, my parents made the same journey for the birth of my sister, Jean.

My father, Clarence Stafford Boyd, was a project engineer for the Florida State Highway Department. As such, he was part of a vast new enterprise to create a national network of paved roads as a result of Congress passing the 1921 Federal Aid Highway Act. Born in 1886, he grew up knowing roads to be either dusty ribbons or muddy mires for wagons and carriages, depending upon the season. But he lived to see the beginning of the transformation of overland travel in America. In 1918, fewer than 8 percent of Americans owned a car. By the end of the next decade, that number had ballooned to 80 percent.

I don't recall my mother, Elizabeth Stephenson Boyd, talking much about my father, or about herself, for that matter. I know only basic facts about her life before my birth. For instance, that she, too, provided me with a legacy in transportation as the granddaughter of John Stephenson, a very successful designer and builder of "railed" coaches.

John Stephenson, born in Ireland in 1809 and brought to America when he was two, founded his own coach-building company at the age of twenty-two. He held patents for the "horse car," a coach on rails pulled by horses. He survived several economic busts and became known as Honest John for always paying his debts. By the time of his death in 1893, the John Stephenson Company of New York had built more than twenty-five thousand streetcars for cities from Saint Petersburg, Russia, to Adelaide, Australia, and from Rio de Janeiro, Brazil, to Bombay, India.

Mother was born in 1888, five years before her grandfather's death, and grew up in a large affluent family on a farm near Great Barrington, Massachusetts. After graduating from a private all-girls school, she earned a degree in nursing from the Pratt Institute in New York. Throughout her life, she proudly made the distinction that she was a "degree nurse."

During World War I, Mother enlisted as an army nurse and worked at the Jefferson Barracks army base in Lemay, Missouri. After the war, she signed up with a friend to work as a nurse in the Panama Canal Zone. During the winter of 1919, they moved to the warmth of Saint Petersburg, Florida, to await their passage to Panama in the spring of 1920. But by the time spring rolled around, Mother had met Father, and the Panama Canal Zone lost a good nurse.

Father was the Pinellas County engineer. He was a competent professional with a good career. I have heard that his mother and his sister, Dora, were not happy about his engagement to my mother. They believed he should marry one of Dora's friends. They did everything they could to dissuade my father. Mother did not take kindly to their opposition.

I have no memory of my father. I was two when he died of an acute asthma attack. By all accounts he was a lively, kind, and good-natured man with a wonderful sense of humor, who was helpful to everyone.

The breach between my mother and my father's family was never rectified. I remember meeting his family only once. I was seven and Jean was six. Mother put us on a train to travel the two hundred miles alone, which was not uncommon in those days, from our home in Macclenny to Saint Petersburg to spend a weekend with our grandmother and aunt. In my seven-year-old memory, they lived together eating an unusual "health diet" consisting of nothing but raw peanuts and honey. Jean and I starved. Exploring the neighborhood, we met a kind Chinese family who gave us chop suey served with rice. We loved it, and I still have a deep appreciation for those generous people.

It might have been the tension between my mother and her in-laws that motivated my parents to leave Pinellas County and move to Macclenny, where they were living when I was born. With Father supervising the work on US Highway 90 between Jacksonville and Lake City, Macclenny, equidistant from the two, made for a convenient place to locate. Father's sudden, tragic death in 1924 left Mother alone in a small town with two very young children.

Mother moved us from Macclenny to Tarpon Springs near Saint Petersburg, to a house my father had owned. We lived there about a year before we became "wanderers." I say that because we went north to live serially with Mother's siblings for a few months at a time. First we lived with Uncle John and his wife, Aunt Etta, who lived north of New York City in Katonah; then with Uncle Dick (his real name was Charles Linley, but he was called Dick) and Aunt Doris near Sheffield, Massachusetts; and then with Uncle Newell and Aunt Margaret near Montreal. In addition we stayed near Stockbridge, Massachusetts, with Mother's only sister and her husband, Aunt Agnes and Uncle Lucius, with whom I spent much more time later in my childhood.

Our wandering ended in 1926 when Mother married Walter Alva Dopson. Walter had been a friend of my parents in Macclenny. I assume Walter pursued Mother by letter until she agreed to marry him. I was four and Jean was three when we journeyed south to our "new" father and our new home.

Macclenny sits in extreme northern Florida, just five miles from the Georgia border. It was a very "Southern" town in both location and attitude. Fifteen miles to the west lay the site of the only major battle of the Civil War fought in Florida. Much of the beef supplied to the Confederate Army came from Florida. Olustee, a crucial stopover for the cattle, was strongly defended by Confederate troops when the Union Army attacked it in February 1864. Losses were high on both sides. The Battle of Olustee ranks as the second-bloodiest battle of the Civil War based on the percentage of Union troops killed and wounded. Union forces fled in defeat, fifty-five miles back to Jacksonville.

During the retreat, a train carrying the wounded Union soldiers broke down ten miles from Jacksonville. This was a potential disaster. Many of the wounded soldiers were black, and Confederate troops were known to kill rather than capture black soldiers. Two African American units, the 54th Massachusetts Volunteer Infantry and the 35th United States Colored Troops, were sent to protect the retreating troops. After defeating the pursuing Confederates, they attached ropes to the broken train and manually hauled it three miles until horses arrived to help them pull it the last seven miles to safety.

Sixty years after the battle, the trenches I played in as a child and the bullets I found buried in the ground were visible remnants of war in that area. The intangible residue of that conflict, however, pervaded the attitudes, behaviors, and culture of the town. It took many years for me to become aware of the influences that were an implicit part of the fabric of my childhood.

In the 1920s, Macclenny, the county seat of Baker County, was a town of about six hundred people, two-thirds white and one-third black. The black population was descended from slaves; the whites were primarily descendants of English settlers who migrated south from the Carolinas and Georgia to become farmers.

The social hierarchy in town was dictated by skin color. There were unwritten rules of conduct for both sides. In some ways there were two separate towns. White residents lived in Macclenny, and black residents lived in what was referred to as "the Quarters." No black resident stayed in town after sundown. A black person meeting a white person on the sidewalk would step off onto the street—even if the white person was a child. The Ku Klux Klan was active in town to "maintain appropriate social behavior." The Klan did occasionally issue warnings to white men who beat their wives or were public drunks, but their primary function was to instill fear in the black population about what would happen if they "got out of line."

The Quarters was made up of small, wooden houses, almost shanties. They lacked running water, electricity, and paint. Most had cheap tin roofs. Before I started school, my sister, Jean, and I would go to the Quarters to play with Aunt Mary's grandchildren.

Aunt Mary was one of the two black women Mother hired to help with housework. Aunt Mary did our ironing. Aunt Mat did the cooking. I don't know why we called them "Aunt." I think it was a generic term, like a white man might call any black man "preacher" if he didn't know his name.

Aunt Mat scared us. She had no patience for kids. If we were running around the kitchen bothering her, she'd say, "If you seez my eyes turn green, I'm gonna keel you!"—and we believed her. She'd cook breakfast, and by the time we were finished eating, she'd have our noon meal, which we called dinner, cooked and waiting on the back of the stove. Mother paid her three dollars a week.

Aunt Mary, on the other hand, was quite sweet. She had two grandchildren the same ages as Jean and me, and sometimes the four of us would play together. Aunt Mary might bring her grandchildren to our house, or sometimes we would walk over to the Quarters. Aunt Mary would sit the four of us down at her small table in the kitchen and feed us lunch, which might include rice, corn bread, turnip or collard greens, and watermelon during the summer. The four of us were good, companionable playmates— until the day we started school, when socializing between the races came to an abrupt end.

The Supreme Court ruling in 1896 mandating that any "separate" education of races be "equal" was only partially obeyed in Baker County. Education for blacks was "separate," but definitely not "equal." There was only one black school in Baker County, and it was a small, run-down, wooden building just outside of Macclenny. There was no playground, and the only school books were well-worn hand-me-downs from the white schools. Ironically, the only person in Baker County with a master's degree, if you didn't count doctors or lawyers, was the black principal of that school.

Macclenny was essentially two and a half blocks of businesses and homes clustered along Highway 90. In such a small town very little went unnoticed. I could be on the street without a soul in sight, yet I knew anything I did would be seen by someone. Folks spent their days sitting in their porch rockers or at their window trying to stay cool, with nothing to do but observe the goings-on.

Many of the services and conveniences taken for granted now did not exist then. There was electricity in town, but every house got its water from its own well. The lucky ones, like my family, had an electric pump to fill their sinks and toilets. Those without electric pumps and indoor plumbing relied on buckets for washing and outhouses in which an old Sears Roebuck or Montgomery Ward catalog served as both reading material and toilet paper.

With no garbage service, most garbage was either buried, burned, or dumped outside the city limits. Our only sources of heat during the cold winters, when the temperature would dip into the 30s, were kerosene heaters, wood-burning stoves, and fireplaces—which were risky since there was no fire department to be called on. If a house or building caught on fire, there was little to do but save what you could before it burned to the ground, a lesson my family learned the hard way.

When I was six years old, Mother was burning newspaper in the fireplace. Some of the burning paper floated up the chimney and settled on the wood-shingled roof. The hot embers set the roof on fire. Jean and I were immediately rushed to safety across the street. We watched as neighbors raced into our house and carried out chairs, dishes, clothes, and anything else they could grab before it was too late. Our house was a total loss. Fortunately, in its place, we were able to build a nice two-story house with fireproof shingles and, for the first time, separate bedrooms for my sister and me.

If the creature comforts were different from today, so was the freedom I enjoyed. I could roam around town by myself or fall in with the other boys and do things like trade marbles or play cowboys and Indians. If we got thirsty, we could knock on any door and ask for a drink of water. There was a big, sprawling camphor tree in the lot next door to our house, and the group of us boys would climb the low, thick branches and sit for hours planning imaginary attacks on imaginary foes.

During hot weather we might walk a mile down Highway 90 to the Little Saint Marys River and swim in the cool, slow-moving, tannin-darkened water. A train whistle might send us running to the depot on the edge of town to see what freight was being delivered. We'd watch men unload canned goods for the grocery store or nails for the hardware store, or wrestle four automobiles out of a just-barely-big-enough boxcar.

The town virtually shut down every Wednesday afternoon. Mr. Brown and Mr. Walker, who owned the hardware store and a wholesale business, respectively, loaded their large flatbed trucks with anyone wanting to take the five-mile ride to the big Saint Marys River. We'd park in a clearing near the river and unload frying pans, fishing rods, and drinks. The gators and the water moccasins seemed to prefer to lie in the hot sun on the Georgia side of the river, avoiding our noisy intrusion into their territory. Gender roles were clear. Women and girls would collect wood and start the cooking fire. Men and boys would go fishing—which I very much liked to do. My favorite was bream. There were also catfish and perch. Eating fresh fried hush puppies and fish on the banks of the river was an enjoyable way for a town to pass a hot summer afternoon.

I was always curious, and my wandering often turned into the occasional odd job. I loved to hang around Jesse Frank Morris's Standard Oil filling station near our house and watch the activity. My first paying job was washing windshields, checking the air in tires, and pumping gas. The pump—taller than a man—had a glass cylinder at the top with markings like a large measuring cup to show the volume of gasoline. I used a hand pump to fill the cylinder with the fifteen-cent-a-gallon gas, which then flowed by gravity from the cylinder into the car. I also worked in the back washing cars, cleaning the inside windows, and, with no vacuum cleaners, sweeping the car floors. Jesse Frank figured a day's work was worth twenty-five cents, and I was glad to have it. A quarter was enough money to go to Jacksonville and pay fifteen cents to see a movie with a dime left over to buy a hamburger and a Coke.

Over one stretch of time, I saved my quarters and bought myself a pair of roller skates, the kind with a leather strap and toe clips that fit over your shoes and were tightened with a skate key. I learned to skate well enough to join my friends as we skated up and down the sidewalks of town, but I never mastered doing tricks or skating backward.

My next paying job was for Mr. Powers, who owned the town hotel, restaurant, barbershop, doctor's office, and drugstore. He regularly hired me to pluck the feathers off a pile of dead chickens for the hotel restaurant. I would dip the chickens in a vat of boiling water and pluck the outer feathers, and then I would singe off the small pinfeathers in the fire. Smelling the wet and the burning chicken feathers, I developed an intense aversion to chicken—an aversion that persists to this day. I liked the money, however, more than I disliked the job. I was relieved when Mr. Powers offered me a job in the drugstore.

The store was managed by Mr. Powers's son, Sid, who lived across the street from the drugstore. When he was sober, Sid was a quiet man who would fill your order at the drugstore without ever saying a word. Every two or three months he would go on a binge and spend several days in bed. If you were nearby, you'd hear him hollering to his wife. "May! Where are you, May? Bring me a drink!"

I remember one time Mrs. Powers invited some of the boys inside and we stood around Sid's bed. He put on a show—jumping out of bed, dancing around in his BVDs, the old-fashioned one-piece underwear with a trapdoor in back. That got us all laughing so hard it hurt.

Although I enjoyed time running around town with friends, I also liked being at home reading or listening to music, two passions I inherited from my mother. I would sit on the living room floor and listen to opera arias on our Victrola, and on Saturday afternoons I'd listen to the New York Metropolitan Opera on the radio. Reading was perhaps my greatest passion. I learned to read at an early age, and there was nothing I'd rather do than read, especially about history. I couldn't get enough.

Most Saturdays, Mother would drive us to the library in Jacksonville. We would wander through the rows of books and pull out ones that caught our interest. Jean and I would return home with as many books as we could carry and race to read through our piles so we could trade books when we finished.

Mother was a voracious reader as well. I remember she liked to read in a wingback chair next to the fireplace. She owned several hundred books, including works by O. Henry and George Bernard Shaw. There was also a twenty-volume History of America, which I read cover to cover the year before I started high school. She had subscriptions to magazines such as the *New Yorker, TIME, Good Housekeeping,* and *Cosmopolitan,* which was a literary magazine at the time. Mother and her friend Emily Taber started the Macclenny Library, which took some effort, because in Macclenny there weren't many people with books to donate—or who had an interest in reading.

Mother had plenty of friends, but she wasn't your typical Macclenny resident. She was an educated, well-read Northerner—and a Republican. Macclenny, as part of the Deep South, was still festering over the Civil War. No self-respecting Southerner would vote for the party of Abraham Lincoln. Everyone in the county knew that Mother was one of only two Republican votes cast in every election. The other vote came from Uncle Tom, the only black resident of Baker County who was allowed to vote.

There were three white schools in Baker County. One was in Macclenny, just on the edge of town. The school had two brick buildings, one for the lower grades and one for the upper grades. There was also a playground, and an auditorium, which was the only place in the county that could accommodate a meeting outside of a church. Each grade, first through twelfth, had its own classroom and teacher.

Every school day, Mother fed us a healthful breakfast and a teaspoon of cod liver oil, quickly washed down with a glass of orange juice. Then Jean and I walked the mile to school with the other kids in town. The farm kids came from the countryside by bus. Early on, Jean skipped a grade ahead into my class. I didn't mind, as Jean and I always got along. Jean was very smart and would help me on the rare occasion that I needed help with schoolwork. I liked school, especially history, and was one of the three top students, the other two being Jean and Mary Estelle Padget.

Every Sunday morning Jean and I got up, put on our good clothes, and walked two doors down the block to the Methodist church for Sunday school, our parents staying behind. I loved the hymns, such as "When the Roll Is Called Up Yonder" and "Just a Closer Walk with Thee." I found the history interesting. I liked learning about Pontius Pilate and the temple priests, and I wondered how Jesus could be, in effect, one of them but an outsider as well. I learned the Bible, too, because every Sunday, every kid had to recite a verse from memory. Always the most popular was John 11:35, "Jesus wept."

I spent most of my childhood avoiding my stepfather, Walter Dopson. I remember Walter as a well-built man, just under six feet, with a stern expression, graying hair, and glasses. As far as I knew, he was completely without a sense of humor. He was a Democrat, because all Southerners were, and a member of the Masonic Lodge. I don't know whether he was a member of the Ku Klux Klan. But one day I did find a white sheet hanging in our coat closet.

Walter was the most successful of the three lawyers in town, representing the local bank, a large turpentine operation, and the county commission. He was also the local attorney for the Seaboard Air Line Railroad. I heard a story that as the railroad's lawyer, my stepfather had a problem during the Depression with the local farmers tying their cows onto the train tracks. Families were desperate for the cash railroads were obligated to pay for cattle killed by trains. To stem the practice, Walter worked out a deal that limited payment to one cow a year per farmer.

People in America today haven't seen poverty on the broad scale we had then. There were no food banks or government programs to help poor and starving families. If help came, it was usually through the churches, where people would give the preacher extra eggs or outgrown clothes to pass around.

I knew kids at school, mostly farm kids, who wore the same frayed shirt and overalls every day, and many of them didn't have even a sweater for the cold weather. Some didn't have shoes and came to school barefoot, the cracks of their feet filled with dirt, looking like a map of the world. In my class, Gussie Mae Johnson wore a dress made from a flour sack, and I'm sure her undergarments were the same.

Nobody was rich in Macclenny, even before the Depression. The only employers of any size were two sawmills, two turpentine companies, and two large nurseries. The nurseries hired only whites, and the turpentine companies hired whites as bosses and blacks as laborers.

Mr. Morris, the father of Jesse Frank Morris, who owned the filling station, was superintendent for one of the turpentine companies. He took a liking to me and would invite me to ride along with him to see what was going on out in the woods and at the turpentine stills. We'd find his crews in the middle of the forest, their mules and wagon nearby, tapping pine trees for sap that was later distilled into turpentine. I'd walk into the woods, curious to study the operation, while Mr. Morris talked to the crew.

Black workers were mostly paid in scrip—essentially a company IOU—and were also given a small amount of cash. The cash was just enough to put something in the collection basket at church on Sunday, buy an occasional hat for the wife, and pay for funeral insurance. I think without exception they all had funeral insurance. Every week a white agent would come to collect the fifteen-cent premium.

The scrip was redeemable only at the company-owned commissary, where the workers purchased everything they ate or wore. The prices were such that they were a little more in debt every month. "Peonage"—the name for this financial trap—was slavery in every sense of the word. There was no way out. If a man tried to leave and look for a job elsewhere, the phone would ring in Macclenny and someone from a sawmill in Nassau County or a turpentine plant in Georgia might say, "I got me a strange nigger here, looks to be 'bout twenty-five, says his name's Charlie Smith. Does he belong to any of y'all?" Charlie Smith would be fetched, beaten, threatened, and put back to work.

I deplore the racist word that was commonly used to refer to a black person. I use it here only to convey the attitudes prevalent in the culture at the time. I grew up around that term and around whites who thought of humans with darker skin as their property. They'd say, "That's my nigger" like you might say, "That's my dog." But that wasn't how Jean and I were raised. Mother treated every person she met with an equal measure of kindness and dignity, and in her quiet way she taught us to do the same.

The commissary of the turpentine company Mr. Morris worked for was in a former showroom of a closed automobile dealership, not far from our house. In the back, in what used to be the mechanics' garage, was a big, round dining room table that served as Mr. Morris's desk. Every Saturday morning the black workers would line up and come in, one by one, to get their pay.

When I was about ten, I was hanging around the commissary on a Saturday morning, as I often did, when one of the workers came in for his pay. Even I could see that he was drunk. He left, but came back about twenty minutes later. "Mr. Morris, you done shorted me my pay," he said.

"I didn't short you, Pete. Now you get outta here and don't be comin' back. I'll shoot you if you do," Mr. Morris warned. Pete shuffled out. A few minutes later he was back. Without a word, Mr. Morris reached into his drawer, pulled out a pistol, and shot Pete in the knee. The worker fell to the floor while Mr. Morris calmly put his pistol back in the drawer and resumed his work. It was a shocking thing to witness. I was so scared that Pete might have been killed that I ran home as fast as I could.

Nobody ever questioned Mr. Morris about the shooting. It was just taken as a matter of course that he had dealt with a problem with one of his workers. Discrimination and inequality were part of the fabric of the community.

Pete wasn't the only person I saw get shot. Baker County was too small to have a full-time judge, so two weeks a year, in the spring and the fall, a judge would visit and hold court. The accused were simply kept in jail until that time. Almost everybody in town showed up to watch the trials, and one day I was outside during a recess when two men got into a fight. One pulled a knife, and the other pulled a gun and shot him dead right there.

There were a lot of farms around Macclenny, most of them sub-sistence farms, providing families with little beyond basic needs. Most farms had one or two mules, and some hogs, milk cows, and chickens. There was no mechanized farming equipment. Everything was done by man or mule. Life on these farms had changed little from the late 1800s, with no running water, tele-phones, or electricity.

Aunt Dona, my stepfather's sister, and her husband, Uncle Giles, had a 160-acre farm about twelve miles out of town. Their farm was larger than most and allowed them to grow some cash crops such as tobacco and cotton. The soil, a pale gray, was mostly sand and not very fertile. The farm was flat, but just beyond it was a pretty little creek with a road that rolled down a slope to where the water flowed. There, a wooden bridge over the creek rattled so loudly that anyone within half a mile knew when a car or wagon was crossing it. During the summers we'd drive out after supper for a visit, which Jean and I loved. We had four cousins there, Giles Jr., who was older, and John, Mary, and Fred, who were about our ages.

Once when I was about eight, we six cousins were hors-ing around with my stepfather's 1930 Dodge sedan, pushing it around the yard, first one way then the other, while our parents sat on the porch visiting.

I was behind the car as it came toward me and I slipped or was inadvertently pushed under the left rear wheel. The car rolled over my belly, across the soft area between my rib cage and hip-bones. It was quick and painless, but I vomited as everything was forced out of my stomach.

Next thing I remember, I was lying in the back of the car being rushed to the doctor's office. A clear set of tread marks ran across my middle. The doctor, finding no damage, thought there was no real concern and sent me home. Fortunately, there was no lasting impact. I don't even think I had to stay in bed long.

For reasons that were never explained to me, Jean and I spent two summers living on the farm with Aunt Dona, Uncle Giles, and our cousins. Maybe my mother was protecting me from my stepfather, or maybe she wanted to give her kids a taste of farm life. Whatever the reason, I got all the taste I wanted.

Everyone at the farm was expected to work. There was always plenty to do. There was the constant upkeep of the place, plus tending to the animals, the crops that fed the animals, the vegetable garden, and the three cash crops: watermelon, tobacco, and cotton. All served to teach me the meaning of "backbreaking" work.

One of my jobs was to pull off the small, unwanted shoots called "suckers" growing around the base of each tobacco plant. I had to be careful not to damage the leaves while stooping over each plant, reaching down to pull the suckers. With the temperature and humidity both in the 90s, sweat gathered on my forehead. I brushed it away with my hand. Soon my eyes started burning. I quickly learned it was ill advised to touch my hot, sweaty face because of the risk of getting nicotine in my eyes. Picking cotton wasn't any more pleasant. With a large sack slung over one shoulder, I had to again stoop to pick the cotton bolls, then drag the sack along, plant after endless plant, down one seemingly endless row after another.

Our free time came in the evening after supper. If there was still daylight, we might play Annie Annie Over, which involved two teams throwing a ball over the house. At the end of the day, we'd gather to sit at Uncle Giles's feet in the living room next to a kerosene lantern. He'd get out his spectacles and read aloud from the Bible before shooing us off to sleep on a warm feather bed, which would have been cozy if it had been winter.

Saturday evening was bath night. The big washtub would be dragged into the living room, and Aunt Dona would fill it half full of water warmed on the woodstove. Uncle Giles went first, then Aunt Dona, and on down the line by age. By my turn, the water was brown, almost muddy.

In spite of everything, I enjoyed my summers on the farm. I liked being with my cousins and spending my days outdoors. But I came home certain in my knowing that farming would have no place in my future.

The dark shadow over my childhood was my relationship with my stepfather. I can't remember a single time I was ever happy to see him. I don't believe he was ever happy to see me, either. I dreaded coming home for dinner. I never knew when I might have done something that angered him.

He did show devotion and respect to my mother. It seemed that they had a good relationship. She would at times plead with him about me, "Oh, Walter, please." But he was good to her, and he had true and genuine affection for my sister. Walter thought the sun rose and set on Jean, for which I'm grateful.

My stepfather was also a good provider. Along with his law practice, he operated an insurance agency out of his office. This was the Depression era, but our family enjoyed a relatively comfortable lifestyle. We had a nice home, decent clothing, plenty to eat, and a newer-model car. I recognized that we never struggled in the way many other families did.

Walter had grown up on a farm about ten miles from Macclenny in a strict Hard-Shell Baptist family. His father was the type of man who did not tolerate disobedience or entertain questions. I believe that my stepfather worked extremely hard to leave the farm and pay his own way through college. He was the first in his family to do so. He failed, however, to leave that severe parenting mind-set behind on the farm—at least when it came to me.

I was an inquisitive kid who wanted things to make sense. I raised questions if they didn't. I would ask my stepfather, "Why do you want me to do this?" or "Why do I have to do it that way?" Maybe he saw this as a contrary streak in me. It also annoyed him that I always fidgeted—as I still do. I can, to this day, hear him say, "Sit still, Alan! Sit up straight!"

I don't think my stepfather went looking for reasons to badger me, but he had strict standards and imposed harsh consequences. Today such treatment might be called abusive. I was certainly fearful around him. If I failed to meet his expectation in the way I split wood for the kitchen stove or swept the walkway, or if I missed one of the insidious sandspurs out in our yard, I could hear the anger in his voice as he lectured me on my failed efforts and made me do it over. I suppose he thought he was doing his duty in raising me to be a "man" the way he had been raised. I never, however, had the sense that he cared for me.

If I failed to heed one of his warnings, or if I got into real trouble, such as when he found me smoking one of his cigars, Walter would march me upstairs to our unfinished bathroom. He kept a razor strop there. A strop is a thick piece of leather about three inches wide and two feet long, used for sharpening straight razors. This one, however, had three small holes bored into it, which made it sting more sharply when it hit me. I was not taken upstairs often, but when I was, Walter wielded that strop with enthusiasm.

When I was about ten years old, after a conflict during supper, my stepfather said, "Come with me!" I remember it was a very dark night. We started walking north out of town. The single streetlight at the end of each block cast a pale circle of light that only made the surrounding darkness more absolute. We passed no one. No cars passed. The only sounds of life came from the night creatures: frogs, mosquitoes, and crickets. It was not cold, but I had no coat, and I shivered as we walked farther up the road that disappeared into the darkness of the forests and swamps of Georgia across the Saint Mary's River.

Pointing into that black emptiness, Walter said, "You have a choice. Either you agree to do everything I tell you to do, or you can just keep walking—and don't come back."

Through tears I told him I would comply.

The walk home was silent except for the insects and my sobs. To this day, that moment stands as the lowest point in my life.

Life continued in a predictable fashion: school, odd jobs, tension at home with my stepfather, until the fall of fourth grade. I was wandering with a friend when we happened upon an open window at the old, abandoned post office. We climbed in to explore, though there wasn't much there. On our way out, my foot slipped and broke a window. Of course someone saw me and told my stepfather.

Walter asked if I knew anything about a broken window at the old post office.

"No," I answered, hoping to avoid trouble.

He slapped my face hard, knocking me across the room. "Don't you ever lie to me again," he said.

During Christmas break a few months later, I was sent away to live with Mother's sister, Aunt Agnes, and her husband, Uncle Lucius, in Stockbridge, Massachusetts. Ten years old, alone on the train from Florida to Massachusetts, most of what I felt was utter relief. For the first time in all the years I had lived with him, Walter's disapproval and anger became a distant thing, left far behind in Macclenny.

II

On the Move

I arrived in New York early in the day and was to leave on another train late in the afternoon. Mother's aunt Grace met me at Pennsylvania Station. She took me in hand and told her chauffeur to drive to Gimbels department store. Riding in a limousine was quite a treat, but walking into a building that could hold the entire town of Macclenny and all of its six hundred residents—and then some—was truly exciting. Aunt Grace told me to pick out anything I wanted. What a daunting challenge! I didn't know so much merchandise existed in the whole world.

Not wanting to look like a country boy, I chose carefully. I left with a baseball and a Boy Scout knife. I thought I did well for my first Christmas shopping at Gimbels. Aunt Grace then took me to the Bronx Zoo, of which she was a trustee. We spent the rest of the day at her large brownstone. I remember it had an elevator and four very entertaining, young Irish maids. By the time Aunt Grace put me on the train to Massachusetts that evening, I thought New York was a wonderful place.

Mother's sister, Agnes, and her husband, Lucius, lived in a small rented house about three miles outside of Stockbridge, near a lake called Stockbridge Bowl. They had two daughters, Betty and Lucia Perrin, called "Hish," but they were both grown and had already left home. The Stockbridge Bowl was a lovely little lake surrounded by a few mansions that were summer homes for the very wealthy.

I remember one place in particular: Shadowbrook Manor. It was enormous. The façade of the house, more than 440 feet long, had castle-like stone turrets and arches stuck in the middle of a huge, rambling English half-timber hunting lodge. At one time it was the longest private dwelling in the United States. Andrew Carnegie owned it until his death there in 1919.

Living with Agnes and Lucius held many pleasures for me. I loved to go exploring. I found some old skis and poles in the garage and taught myself to use them. Caesar, their big Airedale terrier, and I fell in love with each other at first sight. Caesar's heart was as big as he was, which didn't leave him much room for brains. Together, we were intrepid explorers. We would go several hundred feet down the hill, through the maple trees to the shore of the frozen lake, or tromp through waist-deep snow in the woods. I would roam the grounds of the nearby palatial summer homes, which I had all to myself. Looking in the windows, I saw rooms full of furniture draped with sheets.

Aunt Agnes had only two admonitions for my travels: "Don't get lost, and don't be late for supper." The first was almost impossible, as all the land sloped down to the lake, and the second was unthinkable for a healthy ten-year-old boy.

One day Caesar and I happened upon a crew cutting ice on the lake. The ice was probably a couple of feet thick. The workers started near the shore, sawing by hand two parallel cuts several feet apart as they moved toward the center of the lake. Every few feet they would make a perpendicular cut, creating a two-by-two-foot block of ice. Each block was then pushed by poles to shore. The blocks were trucked to the icehouse of the Shadowbrook estate, where, insulated with sawdust, they could last all through the summer.

Uncle Lucius was about five foot nine, a solidly built man with gray hair and a red nose. He was the son of a former governor of New York. By the time I came to live with them, Lucius had worked himself either up—or down—to the position of foreman of a paper mill in the nearby town of Lee. I realized much later that he was an alcoholic. I doubt my aunt had visions of grandeur when she married him, but I came to understand that she was greatly disappointed with the paper mill foreman he had become—kind and good-natured though he was. He would come home "happy," having refueled with a few drinks at a bar after work. He enjoyed teasing "Aggie," sometimes with a ribald joke. To her consternation, she always rose to the bait, saying, "Oh Lucius, oh Lucius!"

I remember Aunt Agnes as white-haired, red-faced, and disheveled. Later I realized she lived a lonely life. With no neighbors or friends, her world revolved around *The Goldbergs,* a popular radio soap opera of the day. Poor Molly Goldberg experienced every misfortune known to humanity. Every afternoon when I arrived home after school, I would find Aunt Agnes sitting at the kitchen table, tears streaming down her cheeks as she suffered through the latest disaster that had befallen Molly. While feeding me an afternoon snack, Agnes would tell me of the challenges Molly was facing. I believe that radio program was about the only pleasure Aunt Agnes had in her life.

Since I was at the end of the school bus route and lived miles from town, I had no opportunity to develop close friendships at the Stockbridge school. My classmates were nevertheless friendly and curious about this newcomer with a Southern accent who joined them in the middle of the year, and were happy to help me learn the new skill of snowball throwing that occupied most of our recess time. I did well in school and enjoyed every class, and I still savor memories of our teacher's encouragement to sing "Funiculi, Funicula" at the top of our lungs.

I was sorry to see that school year end. It meant leaving Aunt Agnes and Uncle Lucius, two decent, good-hearted people who liked me and cared lovingly for me. My time with them remains one of the happiest experiences of my life.

I returned to Macclenny for fifth grade. Striving to be prudent, I sought to keep a low profile around my stepfather. I didn't have to lift my head very high to suffer his wrath.

The next year I was on the road again. I spent sixth grade with Aunt Agnes and Uncle Lucius's daughter Hish. She and her husband, Oliver, lived in Port Chester, New York, a few miles north of New York City. Like her mother, Hish was sweet and kind. Her days, however, were consumed not by Molly Goldberg's life on the radio but by her two small, energetic children. Oliver had a job with the Retail Credit Corporation. It was expected that I would help with chores, and I was assigned the care of the fifty egg-laying chickens kept in the backyard.

The chickens saw me as a source of food and would flock around me as I tried to clean the chicken house. I couldn't do a thing without having to push and kick chickens out of the way. They would squawk and come right back. Their odors brought back my chicken-plucking days.

Hish and Oliver lived in town, so I was able to spend time with the friends I made at school. One classmate was the son of a New York City stockbroker. He shared my curiosity about the world, especially events in foreign countries such as England, France, and even China. We both read the *New York Times* and enjoyed playing games together. Occasionally, in the evening, his father would take us to the local bar and order a martini for himself and a sherry for us. We'd sit at a table and enjoy our drinks, no one thinking a thing of it.

My sixth-grade class in Port Chester afforded me an additional learning opportunity. The girl who sat directly in front of me was black. This was certainly a change from my experience in Macclenny. I was shocked to see her in school. And to my surprise, everyone acted like it was perfectly normal. Watching her raise her hand, speak intelligently, and give good answers was a novel experience for me. Mother had instilled in me the belief that I was not superior or inferior to any person, no matter their race or social standing. Sitting behind this bright, competent girl was clear proof that Mother was right. This prompted me to question the attitudes and the discrimination I'd grown up with back home.

TIME magazine sponsored a current events competition for all the sixth graders in America. The prize was a year's subscription to the magazine. With my love of history and current events, and my regular reading of the *Florida Times Union* back home and the *New York Times* in Port Chester, I was delighted when I had the best score and won the subscription at our school.

Once again, sadly, the school year ended and I was sorry to leave a place where I felt welcomed and liked and had been treated with kindness. I believe Mother was wise to send me to stay with her family. I knew them all well before living with them because nearly every summer we went to New England to visit. Mother knew I would be well treated. I think she realized I had inherited her independent streak. Like her, I enjoyed people, but I enjoyed my own company just as much.

Mother also sought to share her love of travel and adventure with Jean and me. One summer after visiting our New England relatives, we traveled home by ship. We boarded in New York and visited ports all down the coast. I remember seeing Baltimore and Savannah before arriving in Jacksonville. Mother was always eager to give us a wide variety of experiences. Later in her life, she would travel with Jean, and her idea of a successful trip was always to return home with a mind full of memories and less than a dollar in her pocket.

My next two years, during seventh and eighth grades, I lived at home in Macclenny. Staying out of my stepfather's way was my top priority. I went to school, did my chores, and found odd jobs around town to keep me out of the house.

One job required that I get up at four in the morning and go to the Suwannee store. Mr. Cecile, who ran the store, would have me and another boy load his car with corked, empty five-gallon jugs. He would drive us around the countryside and point out bushes where we were to hide them. I would return home by six thirty. I maintained to my parents that I'd been helping a friend deliver newspapers, as I didn't dare let my stepfather know I was helping to supply moonshiners. I think he may have known and not cared—since moonshining was an important local industry.

People claimed Baker County was the Moonshine Capital of the World. That may have been an exaggeration, but brewing liquor was a substantial business in those parts, even after Prohibition ended in 1933. Liquor was a lot cheaper if you didn't pay taxes on it, and jobs and the means to earn cash were scarce during the Depression.

Liquor stills were tucked away in the forests throughout the county. They were always near a source of water, like a creek or a swamp, to provide liquid for the fermenting of the corn mash. A supply of dry wood was necessary to build a fire to heat the still without any smoke that government agents could detect. Baker County stills served markets as far south as Miami Beach and as far north as Atlanta. Our local moonshiners weren't viewed as hillbillies or criminals. They were neighbors and average citizens, practicing what was considered an honorable trade.

By the end of the eighth grade, the tension at home with Walter had become unbearable. Our relationship had deteriorated to the point that Macclenny was no longer big enough for us both. Consequently, I was shipped off to a military school for ninth grade. I was glad for the opportunity to get away from him. The idea of a military academy, wearing a uniform and learning how to drill, also appealed to me.

Gordon Military Academy was in Barnesville, Georgia, about three hundred miles from home. It served as both a military school and as the local town's high school. I shared a room in the barracks with two "good ol' Georgia boys." Every Saturday morning we had inspections. Our underwear had to be properly folded, our clothes hung, shoes shined, and beds made to military precision. If the lieutenant flipped a quarter onto your blanket, it had better bounce. Demerits were passed out for any shortcoming. A demerit brought one hour of marching with a rifle around the drill ground.

I earned a number of inspection demerits early on. One of my failures in life was not paying enough attention to detail. Typically I overlooked something simple. I might leave a pillow hanging out, which delighted the lieutenant. One benefit of having lived with Walter, however, was that I had learned how to follow orders. It didn't take me long to learn the ropes at the academy and how to conform. The officers saw it as their duty to teach me discipline, but, unlike Walter, they had no need to impose their will on me.

In late January I received shocking news. My stepfather had died suddenly from a stroke at the age of fifty-two, leaving Mother widowed a second time. I quickly packed some things, and a family friend, Mr. Gilbert, drove up from Macclenny to take me home for the funeral.

Mother was distraught. She kept repeating over and over again, "Walter's dead, Walter's dead." I'm not sure how Jean felt, since Walter had always been nice to her, but I was absolutely relieved. I did a good job, however, of hiding my feelings. When the funeral was over, I hitchhiked three hundred miles back to the military academy to finish the school year.

I enjoyed that year at Gordon. I made good friends and had several good teachers. It was also during a period when I grew a lot—six inches in two years. Growing is hard work and tiring. As a consequence, I slept through my geometry class almost every afternoon. At the end of the school year my geometry teacher gave me a D. Although I clearly didn't deserve a passing grade, he said he never wanted to watch me sleep through his class again.

That summer, I was hired to help pave the streets of Macclenny, a project funded by the federal government. In preparation for the paving, a bulldozer was used to uncover garbage buried in the dirt roads. The bulldozer crawled along the roads, plowing up nearly a hundred years' worth of embedded tree roots, bedsprings, car parts, and other debris. I walked behind the bulldozer, shoulder to shoulder with other boys. We threw the exposed debris to the side of the road, a road grader following right on our heels, leveling the dirt plowed up by the bulldozer. Positioned between the two machines, we were forced to work at their pace. It was hot, dirty, and tiring work.

We did this ten long hours a day. I dragged myself home every night, dirty and dog-tired. I showered, ate supper, and went to bed, only to get up early the next day and go out and do it all over again. I earned two dollars a day. A loaf of bread cost a nickel, and a fine pair of leather shoes cost four dollars, so that was a lot of money. With no family to support, I saved most of it.

That fall I was scheduled to enter tenth grade. Mother wanted me to start college as soon as possible. She persuaded the principal to advance me into the eleventh grade. I was only fifteen, but the academic year went well. My basketball career, however, could not be deemed as being brilliant. At almost six foot four, I was the tallest boy in school and recruited as the team's center. I think there were only seven boys on the team, as most of the farm kids had already dropped out of school by then. Our team did poorly, lacking talent, skill, and victories.

High school wasn't compulsory back then. It was more of a privilege. My class dwindled from twenty-five in elementary school to sixteen by high school. As a group, we were fairly serious about our studies, and there wasn't much in Macclenny to distract us anyway. There were no school dances. Our movie theater was an old store with a screen and some hard wooden seats. I don't recall anybody asking a girl out, let alone having a girlfriend. I never heard of any of us drinking alcohol. The good Christians of Macclenny frowned on such behavior, and we knew we would be held accountable.

Mother got involved in a new Episcopal mission in town. The two ladies who set up the mission were lively and friendly, and they had a soft sell, which may have appealed to Mother's Congregational roots. Mother, Jean, and I were some of the mission's first members. Early on, the mission consisted of a few of us sitting around discussing the Bible. The discussions led me to ponder such matters as, "Why can you do anything as long as you ask for forgiveness?" Or, "Why is God given credit for all the good, yet not blamed for the bad?" I listened to the others talk, but kept these questions to myself.

Our group slowly grew until we were able to build a charming, small chapel and invite a priest from Jacksonville to come hold Sunday services. Once the priest arrived, the mission lost its appeal for me. I could appreciate the spiritual dimension, but rituals and incantations were something else. "What does that have to do with religion?" I wondered.

Mr. Powers hired me at the drugstore again. I worked everywhere except in the pharmacy area. Stocking shelves, sweeping, cashiering, and manning the soda fountain were just a few of my activities. The soda fountain was typical 1930s-style, with a long marble counter lined with a row of swivel chairs for the customers. When behind the counter, I was a "soda jerk" making fresh-made malts, milk shakes, ice cream sundaes, and sodas. Bottled soda was not yet a common thing.

I also had a stint working at a sandpit about a mile and a half from town, shoveling sand into dump trucks. It was backbreaking work, but it paid good money for a young person like me. Another job involved sitting with a group of middle-aged black men chipping mortar off of used bricks for Mr. Gilbert. I was the only white worker. As a group, we got along well, all of us conforming to the rules of relationship set by the culture. We talked about what was going on in the Quarters, what the preacher had said recently, and thoughts about how long this job would last.

The summer before my senior year I got a job with the Agricultural Adjustment Administration, or AAA, which was established in 1933 to control food prices through crop quotas and subsidies. Fred Robinson and I were a team. Fred was seven or eight years older than me. We'd go out to the fields and measure how much acreage farmers dedicated to each of their various crops, such as tobacco, corn, and watermelons, and we'd report that to the AAA.

Fred and I started most mornings off with a fresh watermelon. After asking permission, we'd go into a field and find a plump, juicy one, cool from the night air, and bust it open, eating only the heart. Then we'd get to work pacing off the fields with a sixty-six-foot chain, the length of four rods, and count the total number of chains for each crop. In the afternoon, we'd find a shady spot to park the car, where we'd sit and sketch out each farm's plantings.

Shade and our straw hats were the only relief we had from the extreme heat and humidity. We also tolerated a lot of mosquitoes, bugs, and lizards, but only a few snakes, which I appreciated, since I don't like snakes. One day out in the field I stepped on a very big black one. I didn't stop to determine what kind it was and took off running faster than I'd ever run before or since. When I looked back, Fred was rolling on the ground in laughter.

"Alan," he said, "you just ran fifty yards and your feet never touched the ground."

The AAA paid me five dollars a day for what I thought was very pleasant work. I enjoyed walking through the countryside, talking to farmers. They were always friendly. They appreciated, too, that Fred and I were very careful in "failing" to notice the occasional still we encountered.

I graduated from high school in 1939. After graduation, about ten of us, along with two teachers, took a Greyhound bus to visit New York City's World's Fair (which remains the second-largest world's fair ever held in the United States). Its theme was The Future, and it comprised four major areas: transportation, government, food, and communication.

I was especially impressed with the transportation area and its Futurama exhibit. Visitors were carried in a chairlift over a

36,000-square-foot diorama of a futuristic section of the United States, showing towns and cities interconnected with a network of highways. This display very much piqued my curiosity. There was also a 3-D movie of a Chrysler being assembled, shown in a theater cooled by a wonderful new invention called air-conditioning.

During my time in New York, my friend John Cruz and I were walking near Times Square when a man approached and offered us the chance to buy a Waltham watch for $15.00. How fortunate we were, for both John and I knew that a Waltham watch was the standard timepiece for the railroads, worth much more than $15.00. We each put up half the price and bought the watch. Later, on the bus home, we opened the box to inspect our prize. We immediately noticed that the hands hadn't moved since we'd purchased it. John wound it, but nothing happened. He then took the back off. There was nothing inside. Relatively speaking, it was a cheap lesson: we each lost $7.50 to learn that if something seems too good to be true, it probably is.

On the way home, we stopped in Washington, DC, where we saw Queen Elizabeth (mother of the current queen) and King George VI of England as they drove down Pennsylvania Avenue. It was the first-ever visit by a king and queen of England to the United States, and one of the highlights of the trip for all of us—especially my classmates who had never been outside of Baker County before.

III

Big Changes

Once back in Macclenny, I again went to work for the AAA measuring crops. I expected it to be yet another typical Southern summer. We had a close family friend, however, Miss Minnie Poythress, who ran a boardinghouse in town for teachers. In July, just after my seventeenth birthday, Miss Minnie called my mother and asked if I could pick up a new teacher arriving on the afternoon train. I was happy to oblige. And was glad I did. That was the afternoon I first laid eyes on Flavil Townsend. Slim and pretty, she stood about five foot four with freckles and blue eyes. Flavil had graduated only that morning from Florida State College for Women in Tallahassee (now Florida State University), and had taken a job teaching home economics at Taylor High School, just twelve miles down the road from Macclenny.

Flavil had grown up about sixty miles from Macclenny on a farm on the banks of the Suwannee River. Her family was what was called Hard-Shell or conservative Baptists, who did not tolerate drinking or dancing. They attended church every Sunday morning and evening, and prayer service on Wednesday evenings as well.

I immediately liked her. She was easy to talk to. I would learn in time that she had grown up the youngest of seven children and had been not quite two when her mother died. For a time, she was sent to live with her grandmother. Her father soon remarried, and it was not long before Flavil became the seventh of eight children. With a baby to care for, her stepmother had little time for—or interest in—Flavil. Fortunately her brothers and sister loved her and cared for her. When her father died a few years later, her stepmother left the family. Ten-year-old Flavil was then raised by her brothers and sister. Her oldest brother, William, dropped out of college, got a job with the post office, and dedicated himself to keeping the family together. He also put most of them through college—this even in the midst of the Depression.

It was only after several months that I began to truly spend time with Flavil. We discovered that we both liked to read and to talk about books. At the time, she didn't realize I was four years her junior, given my height. And I wasn't in a hurry to tell her. To my advantage, the slim pickings of eligible men who read books in Macclenny helped me finagle time with her that first summer.

One night she gave me a long dissertation about Nietzsche, which I found fascinating. She had an opinion on just about everything—and felt compelled to share it. She was lively and intelligent, but sometimes, in my view, too quick to judge. Nevertheless, we shared a passion to understand, explore, and travel the world.

We did have our differences. She was light-footed and a graceful dancer; I had two left feet. We differed on music as well. Flavil liked popular music, whereas I preferred classical. Happily, she overlooked my faults, and our relationship blossomed. That fall I left to begin my freshman year at the University of Florida in Gainesville. But on weekends I would take my laundry and hitchhike the sixty-five miles home to enjoy her infectious laugh and quick mind.

I enjoyed college from the start. At school, I wore the "rat cap"—like every other freshman, a bright orange ball cap with a bright blue "UF 43" emblazoned across the front. And though I wasn't a football fan, I supported our Gators and never missed a home game. Though the Florida football team had lost every game, we were still enthusiastic and hopeful. We referred to the string of losses as "unwon" games.

One weekend, a friend suggested that we hitchhike 350 miles north to cheer on our winless football team against the awesome, undefeated Georgia Tech team. Wearing our student rat caps, it was easy to get rides to Atlanta. To our utter amazement, the Gators won 16 to 7. We left the stadium in a vibrantly happy mood, well inebriated from a smuggled flask of bourbon.

Walking through downtown Atlanta, we saw that the Andrews Sisters, the most popular singing group in the country, were performing at the Fox Theatre. We bought tickets for the show. Encouraged by a few more drinks, I decided to sing along from my balcony seat. It wasn't long before an usher invited me to continue my rendition of the songs out on the street.

That night, as we waited for a ride back to Florida, proudly wearing our rat caps, a police car suddenly pulled up. The officer, clearly a Georgia Tech fan, pointed out that we were still within the Atlanta city limits. "If you bastards aren't out of the city within fifteen minutes, I'm going to put you UNDER the jail!"

We quickly walked beyond the city limits and got a ride forty miles to Griffin, Georgia. It was too late and too dark to hitchhike farther. We found an unlocked car on a used car lot, crawled inside, and went to sleep. Otherwise, it was an uneventful trip home. Back on campus Sunday evening, no one seemed especially impressed by my performance at the Fox Theatre with the Andrews Sisters. Not a soul asked for my autograph.

The University of Florida was a good fit for me. I spent a fair amount of time in the library, which held the biggest collection of books I'd ever seen. I loved to wander around and look at all the different volumes, amazed that so many could be in one place. While at UF, I went to my first ballet performance. I worked out at my first gym. I'd never seen or heard of a gym before, and I took an instant liking to the weights, the exercise equipment, and even the climbing rope.

Nothing had a greater effect on me, though, than my freshman political science class. It was my good fortune to take a class taught by Professor William "Wild Bill" Carleton. He could have been a Shakespearean actor. He walked, paraded, and stalked back and forth, waving his arms and undulating his voice while outlining how our federal government worked. He made clear how laws were made and how things got done. He held the US Constitution in utter reverence. His discussion of the legislative powers was vivid. His discussion of the contest of ideas in the political process was joyful. He brought governance to life without revealing his political leaning one way or the other.

Professor Carleton inspired me. He melded my innate curiosity about current events with the nuts and bolts of our political process. He, more than anyone, sparked my lifelong interest in government. It was a pleasure and a privilege to be his student. Words fail me as I try to convey his grandeur as a human and his significance in my life.

At the end of my freshman year, the summer of 1940, I followed Flavil to Jacksonville. She had found a summer job with

the Southern Bell Telephone Company as a comptometer operator. A comptometer is a type of adding machine. She lived with
her college roommate in a small apartment at the rear of a house
owned by her brother William. I rented a room about four blocks
away.

That summer I worked for Sears Roebuck repairing Cold-
spot refrigerator freezers. We had a quota of so many units per
day and so many per week, and if we beat the quota, we'd get
a bonus in addition to our wage of thirty-five cents an hour. It
wasn't difficult work, but spending my days on the second floor
of a warehouse with no ventilation in high heat and humidity was
enervating. After work I'd go home, take a bath, and then go over
to Flavil's for supper. We spent most evenings together talking
and walking. Sometimes we'd go to a movie.

Her brother William was an elder in the Jacksonville Main
Street Baptist Church. He was a true Christian in every sense of
the word. He helped Flavil get into college and even paid for part
of it. She was very fond of him and looked up to him as a father
figure.

Flavil was an atheist, but she kept that from William, not
wanting to hurt his feelings. To please him once, she attended a
revival at his church, and I went along to keep her company. We
sat together in the balcony as the preacher, Hyman Appleman,
spewed a message of hell and damnation, calling followers to
come forward to be saved. As the congregation sang "Almost
Persuaded," a few staggered forward. At the beginning of the
fourth verse, Mr. Appleman raised his eyes to the balcony and
pointed right at me.

"I will give you one last chance to be saved!" he commanded.

The spectacle of one human assuming that he was better than
another, and capable of guaranteeing salvation, was too much for
me, and I told Flavil so. We got up and left. I knew it would not

set well with William, but I would not tolerate another man telling me he possessed the power to save me.

My freshman year was paid for by five shares of General Motors and five of Montgomery Ward stock, left to me by Uncle Billy, my mother's brother. That largesse was exhausted by the start of my sophomore year, which meant that I would have to work to pay the nine-hundred-dollar tuition plus the cost of room and board. Mother would have helped if she'd been able to, but she had her own struggles.

When Walter died, he'd left her all that he'd owned. This included our home, a house next door, a car, his law practice, and the property insurance agency. He also left her his law books and office furniture. This left her with assets but no income, which meant she had to suddenly figure out how to make money. Deciding she would run the insurance agency, she got her insurance license and moved the insurance business into her home.

Mother also decided to become a landlord. She sold the law books and office furniture, and used the money to convert the garage behind the house into a duplex. She turned the back porch into her bedroom and made the upstairs of the house into a separate apartment with access from outside. To better accommodate the insurance business, she added a room onto the side of the house. Mother proved her resourcefulness by managing all of this on her own. Later, she also had another duplex built on the lot next door that Walter had purchased before his death.

In the fall of 1940, I started my sophomore year at the University of Florida and also a job at Camp Blanding, an army training base being built twenty-five miles from Gainesville. I was a timekeeper for a construction company that was building roads and bridges on the base. Monday through Friday, I commuted with four other students to Camp Blanding to work a shift from late afternoon until midnight. Sharing one car meant that no one could leave until everyone was ready to go. I typically didn't get home before 1:30 a.m.

My choice of college courses my second year proved to be less than ideal. I enrolled in an eight-credit-hour accounting course that met at eight in the morning. Some mornings I simply couldn't get out of bed in time for class. A large part of the grade was based on compiling a complete set of accounting books for an imaginary small business. This was a very time-consuming task. At the end of the term I had no completed set of books to turn in. I failed the class. Despite my shortcomings with regard to attendance and failure to develop accounting records, I felt cheated: I had clearly demonstrated my understanding of the course by scoring a 96 on the final exam.

Another rather poor choice was a class in statistics. I did not understand the theory, or I failed to focus, because I received an F in that class as well. The professor's parting comment to me was, "Boyd, you are the dumbest white man I've ever known." Clearly, racism was capable of permeating the halls of academia.

At the end of the school year I was called into the administrative office to talk to the dean. He got right to the point. "I am confident," he said, "that the university is sufficiently strong that it can survive without you. Good luck—and don't come back."

Though this was not a surprise, I was sorry to hear it. Still, I was undaunted. I figured that I'd be back in college again someday, maybe as a history professor. Mother, to her credit, was more sympathetic than I probably deserved. She thought correctly that my job at Camp Blanding was too much for me.

With my dismissal from college, I moved to Starke, just six miles from Camp Blanding. I took a full-time position with the same construction company. Ironically, my new title was book-keeper and assistant superintendent. I was responsible for tracking everything from hours worked to gasoline consumed and materials installed. I recorded supplies, lumber, and gravel on a daily basis. And at times I was called upon to do routine labor. One such job was to help carry sixty-six-pound bags of cement, one on each shoulder, from a railcar to a transport truck. I never objected to the physical labor required, though I can't say I looked forward to it either.

I liked both the job and the money. I was paid $75.00 a week, which was a solid middle class income even for a family. I also had use of a company truck. My room cost me a dollar a day, and I paid $1.25 a day for three big meals. I felt as rich as Croesus, and put most of my money into savings.

That September, Flavil left for the University of Tennessee in Knoxville, 550 miles away. She had enrolled to earn her master's degree in home economics with a minor in child psychology. We regularly wrote each other, and I spent some of my money going up to Knoxville to see her a couple of weekends in the fall of 1941. We never talked on the phone, as phone calls were very expensive. The only long-distance calls were for emergencies and went something like, "I'm sorry to say that your mama's dead."

I got to know some of the infantry recruits at Camp Blanding while working construction on the base. I went on a few bivouac exercises with them, ending up wondering why the hell anyone would choose to march all day while wearing a pack, eat K-rations, and sleep on the ground with bugs and snakes. "No thank you," I thought to myself.

One Sunday afternoon in early December, I was alone in my construction shack putting together the monthly report. The radio was playing in the background. Suddenly the announcer interrupted the broadcast. His urgent tone caught my attention.

The day was December 7, 1941. The Japanese had attacked Pearl Harbor.

Having worked in and around Camp Blanding for almost two years, I had had ample experience with the life of an infantry soldier. I resolved right then and there to take a company truck first thing in the morning and drive to Jacksonville to make my preparations for the war.

The next morning, I was first in line at the Army Air Corps recruiting office to sign up as an aviation cadet. The Army Air Corps required at least two years of college to qualify. I could honestly assert that I had attended two years of college. Passing or failing proved not as significant an issue for the army as it had been for the University of Florida. I was immediately sworn in and told to return to my work to await further notification.

President Franklin D. Roosevelt declared war against Japan that day. Three days later, on December 11, war was declared against Germany. War, in fact, had been a continuous topic of conversation for more than a year. I and most everyone I knew hadn't given it much serious thought, thinking that our fathers had fought in World War I, and that if Europe screwed things up again, that was their problem. We believed ourselves to be pacifists. Japanese aggression toward China and other distant countries were topics of discussion, but none of us imagined that Japan would attack our shores. Once they did, however, things changed dramatically. We all fell into a fervor to sign up and fight. Every young man in my boardinghouse and all of my pacifist friends from school ended up enlisting.

IV

War Preparation

I was told to report to Camp Blanding in March 1942 as one of about five hundred aviation cadets. Camp Blanding, being an infantry base, seemed to have no program for training us for the air corps. To give us something to do, we were assigned to inventory the motor vehicle pools.

Eager to do our part in the war effort, my team counted every nut, bolt, radiator cap, and spare tire. Our task was completed in a few days. Again we had nothing to do. To keep us busy, we were ordered to change areas and inventory an area that had just been counted by another team. Eventually, wiser heads prevailed. We were sent on leave and told that we would receive a telegram ordering our return once there was space for us in the Air Corps training system. We were instructed to ensure that our local Western Union office knew how to reach us.

Mother suggested we drive to New England to visit her family. I would have no chance to see them again until after the war. Flavil came, too, as she was nearly family by this time. The question was not would we marry, but when?

I took our travel itinerary with addresses and telephone numbers to the railroad station agent in Macclenny, who was the Western Union operator as well. She knew me and agreed to contact me as soon as the wire ordering me to report arrived. Mother, Jean, Flavil, and I drove north in Mother's 1940 Chevrolet coupe. Our first destination was Stockbridge, Massachusetts, to visit Aunt Agnes and Uncle Lucius, who now lived in town.

On Sunday afternoon, our second day there, a heavy thunderstorm swept into town. I went into the living room to close a window. The tall pine tree next to the house held an aerial wire that ran through the window to the radio. I remember reaching up to close the window. My next memories are of feeling warm in a pleasant space, listening to soft music, while figures dressed in white quietly moved around. I was filled with a sense of peace and comfort that I was reluctant to leave.

Returning to consciousness brought pain. I was lying on my back on the floor, across the room from the window. A man was kneeling by me, giving me artificial respiration. He was a doctor who lived two doors away. I was fortunate it was a Sunday and the doctor was home. I was told I was unconscious almost thirty minutes.

Apparently, at the moment I reached up to close the window, lightning struck the tree, traveled down the radio aerial, and jumped to me, burning the hair on the left side of my head where it made contact. It ripped my shirtsleeve, traveled down through my body, ripped the bottom of my trouser leg, and burned a hole in the wooden floor where I had been standing.

Every joint in my body hurt. My pulse was 170. An ambulance rushed me to a hospital in Great Barrington. A day later I left the hospital with my heart rate still at 170, ordered to take the digitalis pills given me to slow my heart rate. I had lost seventeen pounds in one day. At 150 pounds, I was a six-foot, four-inch scarecrow. We soon said our goodbyes to Aunt Agnes and Uncle Lucius and started the long drive back to Florida.

When we arrived home in the late afternoon several days later, a neighbor told me that the military police had been to the house looking for me. The Western Union wire ordering me back to Camp Blanding had come while we were away. But my friend at the Western Union office had failed to inform me. I was now being sought as a deserter.

I returned to camp the next morning. Entering the commanding general's office, I saw that perhaps good fortune was on my side. Betty Green, a friend and schoolmate, was the commanding general's secretary. She greeted me warmly. "Alan, where the hell have you been?"

I showed her the letter from the doctor in Stockbridge documenting the lightning strike and hospitalization. Betty told me to sit down and not move. She took the letter in to the general. A moment later she returned to tell me that I needed to be on a train that evening heading to Kelly Field in San Antonio, Texas.

Flavil, Mother, and Jean all met me when the train passed through Macclenny, so we were able to say our goodbyes. Mother handed me a suitcase packed with clothes. I later found that she'd slipped in ten dollars as well.

The good news was that I would be on a train instead of in the brig. The bad news was that when I reached Kelly Field, I would be given a physical like all cadets to qualify me for flight training. If I failed, I'd be shipped off as a private for less pleasant duty. My pulse was still too high and my weight still too low to qualify for flight training.

My luck continued to hold on the train. Pullman sleeping cars in 1942 had no air-conditioning, and doors at the ends of the cars were left open during warm weather to provide fresh air. Assigned to a lower berth on the aisle for the overnight ride to New Orleans, I was hot and sweating. A fierce breeze roared over me all night. In the morning I awoke with terrible pain in my chest. I was so sick and feverish, I couldn't get out of bed. When the train arrived in New Orleans, I was taken by ambulance to LaGarde General Hospital, an army hospital on the shores of Lake Pontchartrain, where I was admitted.

The diagnosis was pleurisy. With my chest tightly wrapped, I was put in a private room in the officers' ward. Fortunately, that early in the war, the hospital didn't know that an aviation cadet was not yet an officer. I slept for forty hours straight, and woke up feeling healthy and hungry.

LaGarde was still governed by prewar army regulations. Anyone admitted to the hospital could not be discharged until the retirement board reviewed his case. The local retirement board met only once a month, and had met just three days before my arrival. So I had to stay in the hospital with nothing to do but get healthy. It provided a lovely, month-long vacation in New Orleans.

Another patient, an army chaplain, and I became good friends. We routinely received day passes to leave the hospital. In a park on Lake Pontchartrain near the hospital, a number of shacks sold all-you-could-eat boiled shrimp for fifteen cents. Another fifteen cents bought a Jack's beer to wash them down.

We often went to the French Quarter to listen to music and enjoy meals in the city's wonderful restaurants. This helped put back the weight I'd lost. Every evening at the hospital I could also eat all I wanted. And at bedtime, a nurse would bring me a malted milk shake the doctors had prescribed as part of my regimen for recovery. Though I gained weight, my pulse was still elevated. Secretly I continued to take my digitalis pills. At the end of the month when the retirement board met again, I was declared fit to continue my journey.

I boarded the train to San Antonio with mixed feelings, eager to become a pilot, yet sad to say goodbye to my new friend and to the pleasant interlude we'd enjoyed. I also still feared that I might fail the physical and end up in the infantry, because my heart rate was still above the allowable limit for pilots.

When I finally arrived at Kelly Field in San Antonio, the place was overrun with cadets. There was no space for me in the barracks, so I was assigned to the "tent city." In a crowded six-man tent with a single lightbulb and a wooden floor, I awaited with dread the physical and psychological tests I feared would come at any moment.

Once again I had a little luck. Although a Florida native, I had never in my life encountered a hurricane. The day after I arrived in Texas, a hurricane blew through.

There was a real danger the planes would be damaged by the wind, particularly the AT-6 single-engine advanced training planes. They had no tie-downs or control locks. Some AT-6s had been flown to safety, but all of the flight cadets were ordered out into the storm, a cadet on each wing, with one cadet in the cockpit to hold the controls of those that remained.

In my weakened state, I knew where I needed to be. I was inside the glass-covered cockpit before the other two cadets had time to think. I held the controls, protected from the elements, as the storm ravaged the base.

Kelly Field was a mess. Every tent in camp had been blown down. Amazingly, the base was back up and running on schedule again in two days. The storm, however, had graced me with two additional days of taking digitalis.

Once things were operational, we flight cadets lined up for our tests. There were psychological and coordination tests in addition to the physical. Coordination testing involved two record players spinning side by side in opposite directions. I had to track both turntables at the same time with a wand.

Part of the physical involved standing in a long, single-file line to get vaccinations. When your turn came, you were hit with needles from both sides. The guy in front of me fainted. That ended his aviation career. I felt sorry for him and hoped to God that wouldn't happen to me.

The most nerve-racking part of the physical for me was waiting to meet the doctor and his stethoscope at the end of the line. I had no idea what he'd find or if I would pass. My pulse rate, the doctor found, was 95, just at the upper limit of the acceptable range. All the shrimp, fine dinners in New Orleans, and nightly milk shakes I'd had to suffer paid off. My weight broke just above the lower limit. I passed.

Late that night, I quietly went out to the dark parade ground, scraped the label off the digitalis bottle, chewed it up, and swallowed. Digging a hole in the ground with my heel, I crushed the bottle, buried it—and never looked back.

Those of us who passed all the tests became aviation cadets. We moved into the barracks and were issued a footlocker and uniforms, including regulation underwear, socks, and shoes. We immediately started intensive physical training. We attended ground school, where we learned about army life and some aviation basics. We were told that our flight training would be divided into three sections, Primary, Basic, and Advanced, with each running about three months.

After a few weeks of ground school, I was assigned with a group of one hundred cadets to Muskogee, Oklahoma, to begin Primary Training. We were members of the class of 43E, scheduled to graduate as pilots in May 1943.

Heading for Muskogee, I thought about my journey to become a cadet. I'd been struck by lightning, hunted as a deserter, hospitalized with pleurisy, and hit by a hurricane. I figured things couldn't get worse.

Muskogee Army Airfield had been a civilian airport called Hatbox Field before the army turned it into a Primary Training base and contracted with a local aviation school to train cadets. My instructor, a kind, considerate, thoughtful man, was an excellent communicator. Before the war he had been a recreational pilot. His previous employment was as the piano player for the band that played for the *Grand Ole Opry,* the Saturday night radio program. He was a delightful teacher.

We trained in groups of six on the Fairchild PT-19 trainer. It was a rudimentary plane with a maximum speed of 124 mph and two open cockpits, one forward for the instructor and one rear for the student. A Gosport tube—basically a pipe between the two cockpits—was used for communication. Instructor and student each wore an earpiece and shouted into the funnel, hoping to be heard.

I had never flown before. I'd seen only one small plane up close, and that was on the ground. The morning of my first flight I was excited. My instructor went over the flight plan. The objective was for me to feel what it was like to be up in the air.

When the plane lifted off the ground, I experienced the greatest sense of exhilaration I had ever known. It never occurred to me to be afraid. The moment of sheer ecstasy was beyond description. As we gained altitude, I was transported into a different world. Looking down I saw houses, streets, and fields from a new perspective. In the open cockpit, wind rushing by me, I felt free, soaring like a bird, unrestricted by the roads, fences, and buildings below.

The instructor turned the controls over to me. I felt the plane respond, turning right as I pushed the right rudder, ascending when I pulled the stick back. We climbed to about five thousand feet. We flew no more than twenty-five or thirty minutes, but it was long enough to make me feel like a new man. I was hooked.

In Primary Training we learned the basics of flying: how to take off and land; how to recover from spins and stalls. Our most challenging test was the first solo flight. But I didn't find that difficult, because flying came easily to me. I loved it. Primary Training was pure pleasure. The time in Muskogee was wonderful.

After completing Primary, we transferred as a group to Strother Field in Winfield, Kansas, for Basic Training. The airfield had been under construction as a civilian airport before the war. The Army Air Corps took it over, changed the name to Strother Army Airfield, and rushed to complete its construction. Arriving in the middle of November, we moved into barracks that, still under construction, had no heat. It was so cold that we slept in our full winter flying suits: fur-lined leather pants, jacket, gloves, and cap with earflaps.

We learned the basics of instrument flying in a simulator. The simulator was an exact replica of the real Vultee BT-13s we were to fly. The Vultee BT-13 was similar to the PT-19 we had flown in Basic, but had an enclosed cockpit. What we practiced in the simulator we would try to master in the plane. On early flights, we'd be accompanied by an instructor who coached and evaluated us.

We started acrobatic training, learning loops, snap rolls, slow rolls, and chandelles, which are 180-degree banked turns. Occasionally, cadets would get queasy from the turning and twisting. Sometimes they'd throw up in the cockpit. No one thought anything of it, so long as cadets cleaned up their own mess with a bucket of water and rags upon landing.

Our flight instructor, a new second lieutenant, didn't have many more flying hours than we did. He was short, five foot six at most. I was the tallest of the six men in our flight. I was always polite to him and addressed him as "sir." I followed his instructions and never acted like a smartass. Yet he remained cold and distant toward me. He appeared to have an intense dislike of me for no reason I could understand. As the weeks wore on, he seemed personally set against me.

One day I was on the ramp, next in line for a flight. The plane landed, and I could see that Cadet Behnken had thrown up all over the rear trainee cockpit. He climbed out and headed toward the cleaning supplies. The lieutenant, looking down, saw that I was next.

"Never mind that, Behnken," he commanded. "Boyd, get in the cockpit. Now!"

Behnken protested. "Lieutenant, I need to clean up the mess first."

"Get away from the plane, Behnken. Boyd, get in the cockpit!"

Behnken had no choice but to stand down. I climbed up into the vomit-filled cockpit. The lieutenant took the controls and we were off. He flew us over the Kansas fields doing loop after loop. After our fourth loop, knowing that vomit was sloshing all around me, he asked, "Are you sick yet, Boyd?"

"No, sir."

He continued doing loops and rolls, all the while calling out, "Are you sick yet, Boyd?"

I wasn't. I was determined I would choke before giving him the satisfaction of making me throw up. Finally realizing I was not prone to motion sickness, he gave up and returned to base.

After we landed, he said he was "washing me out." He said I wasn't a competent pilot. That meant the end to my career as a pilot. Shocked, I pleaded my case, but he was relentless and determined to get rid of me.

Fortunately, the army had invested a significant amount of time and money in my training as a cadet. As was policy, no one was ever washed out of Basic without a second opinion. A different flight instructor was assigned to test my flying skills. My review flight was scheduled for the following day.

I didn't sleep much that night, wondering what I'd done wrong. Thinking that one flight now stood between me and the infantry pushed sleep completely aside. The next day, I stayed calm throughout the test flight. I went through the paces with the new officer in the instructor's seat. We landed, taxied, and parked.

"Boyd, there's nothing wrong with the way you fly," the officer said to me. "What's going on here?"

I told him the story, about the endless loops and the cockpit filled with effluvium.

"You're not going anywhere," he said. "Naturally, we'll assign you another instructor for the balance of your time here."

I was happy to complete Basic as a member of another group.

For Advanced Training, some pilots went for more single-engine training, and others, like myself, learned how to fly twin-engine aircraft. As a consequence, I was sent to the Altus Army Air Base in Altus, Oklahoma.

At Altus, we had two types of twin-engine training planes, the Cessna AT-17 and the Curtis AT-9. We first learned the rudiments of twin-engine flying, like what to do if one engine failed and how to use a variable speed propeller. Then most of our flying became instrument flight, night flight, and cross-country navigation, all of which I enjoyed. Our navigational tools were limited. To get our bearings we had a compass, a map, and landmarks. If we got lost, we would look for train tracks. Train tracks always headed toward towns. Every town had a water tower with the town's name painted on it. We all came to think of water towers as our best friend.

Shortly after arriving at Altus, I was honored to be appointed as cadet corps adjutant. Within the cadet corps, the top-ranking job was cadet commandant. The number two job was cadet corps adjutant. I didn't receive any more pay or have more power, but I did get to march at the head of the group, one step in back of and to the left of the cadet commandant.

Now confident that I would get my wings and second lieutenant bars, and believing that I'd be sent overseas soon, Flavil and I decided it was time to get married. She had been teaching kindergarten in Jacksonville while living with her sister, Geneva. She now made her arrangements to join me.

Flavil told her brother William. "Alan asked me to marry him," she said. "What do you think?"

"Well," William started, "as far as I know, Alan is a good boy. Two things I know wrong about him. Number one, he smokes. Number two, he's a member of a church that is next to the church of the devil himself."

William referred to the fact that I had attended an Episcopal church, which some considered close kin to the Catholic Church. Baptists in the South were strongly anti-Catholic. In spite of my "faults," William did not oppose our marriage.

Mother had always liked Flavil—until we decided to get married. Suddenly, she decided that Flavil was too old for me. I believe it was a "She's not good enough for my boy" response. I was disappointed Mother fell into that trap. Flavil and I, focusing only on each other, didn't let anyone change our minds. Time proved us right.

Flavil was unable to take the train from Jacksonville to Altus since every train was filled with soldiers moving around the country. Instead, her 1,200-mile journey involved enduring multiple crowded buses, one after another. Sometimes she had to sit on the steps at the front of the bus, certainly an act of true love. I met her last bus on Saturday, March 27. We walked to the Altus Hotel, the only one in town, and checked her in.

On Monday, the 29th, we got our marriage license, and Flavil, a trained and experienced teacher, then went to the local school and was hired on the spot.

On Saturday, April 3, 1943, Flavil and I were married in a small chapel on the base, along with two cadet friends and their fiancées. That evening, the six of us shared our wedding dinners at the Altus Hotel.

Cadets were required to sleep on base every night. I, however, got in the habit of spending Saturday and Sunday nights at the hotel with Flavil. One Monday morning, I stopped at a little restaurant in town for breakfast before my return to the base. After taking a seat at the counter, I noticed that the commandant of cadets was sitting on the stool next to me. Before the war he had been a teacher in Jacksonville. He knew Macclenny well, and we had shared several pleasant conversations about home. As he had always been in the past, he was most pleasant to me.

When we finished eating, he asked me, "Would you like a ride to the base?"

"Yes, sir," I answered.

We got into his car and set out. "You know what I've got to do, don't you?" he asked as we drove toward the base.

"Yes, sir."

Later that day, by his order, I was busted as the cadet corps adjutant. It was a fair trade. The time with Flavil was worth it.

The balance of my time in Advanced was uneventful. When I was commissioned, Flavil pinned me with my wings and my second lieutenant bars, a proud moment for both of us. I was then assigned to become a troop carrier pilot.

Because I'd been given a short leave before I had to report to my next post, Flavil and I made a brief visit home to Macclenny before moving to Austin, Texas, where I was trained to fly DC-3s and C-47s. They were basically the same plane, one civilian and the other military. They were reliable, enjoyable planes to fly. My transition to troop carrier pilot was easy.

Flavil and I were living together for the first time, so Austin was like a honeymoon. We rented a nice room from a hospitable couple. We also learned about the delights of Tex-Mex food. While in Austin I received my assignment to the 82nd squadron of the 436th Troop Carrier Group, which would be my unit for the duration of the war.

The 436th was composed of four squadrons, the 79th through the 82nd. It was being assembled in Alliance, Nebraska, and made up of personnel from all over the country. By the time I arrived, two-thirds of the squadron had been assigned to their planes. I became copilot to one of the early arrivals, a wonderful fellow from Wyoming named Hal Woodard. Woody and I spent almost every day, all day long, flying together. We flew formations, practiced cross-wind landings, and learned how to take off with and tow gliders.

Two months later, our outfit was transferred to Laurinburg-Maxton Air Base in North Carolina. Our time there was spent flying formations, day and night, as well as towing gliders—again, both day and night. We learned to tow single gliders as well as two gliders at a time. This was tricky, because C-47s take off at 95 miles per hour—but stall at 94 mph. There was no room for error when pulling a glider.

Occasionally we would be assigned to spend a day at nearby Camp McCall or Fort Benning, Georgia. Paratroopers were required to make five qualifying jumps to be certified. Our role was to pick them up, drop them, then return to pick up another group. C-47s could carry twenty-one passengers, twenty trainees plus a jumpmaster. Paratroopers had a hook that they attached to an overhead cable that ran the length of the plane; the other end of the hook was fastened to their parachute rip cord so that when they left the plane, their parachute pins were automatically pulled and their chutes would open. The jumpmaster was positioned opposite the open door. Any trainee who froze was encouraged to jump by a large boot that sent him out the door in a hurry. These flights were routine for pilots, so much so that often one of us would watch the jump procedure from the cockpit door. What a sight!

Flying over North Carolina in autumn was beautiful. We were close to the Blue Ridge Mountains, where the foliage changed daily. I remember that the oranges, reds, and golds were spectacular.

Two individual flights from this time stand out as especially memorable. Once, my pilot and I were sent on an errand from North Carolina to Dover Army Air Base in Delaware, late in the day, after what had already been a very long, tiring day of flying. It was after 9:00 p.m. when we finally left Dover Air Base to fly home. We had not had time to eat. Tired, hungry, with calm weather and a dark night ahead of us, we turned on the autopilot. Unfortunately we both fell asleep.

We awoke with light flooding our cockpit. A fighter plane was roaring directly at us with its lights on. Startled, I looked around to get our bearings. We were over Washington, DC, in a restricted zone directly above the White House. We quickly course corrected. The fighter plane no doubt was prepared, if necessary, to shoot us down. Fortunately, the pilot merely reported our serial number.

We did not sleep the rest of the trip. When we landed in North Carolina, Colonel Williams, the group commanding officer, was waiting. "What the hell were you doing?" he barked.

The only thing we could do was tell the truth. He berated us at considerable length, but didn't put anything in our records. That was as good an ending as we could expect as far as I was concerned.

The other experience was more calamitous. Shortly before we were shipped overseas in December, I was assigned to fly a group of enlisted men to Pittsburgh for a weekend at home with their families. On Sunday night we took off after dark, heading back to North Carolina.

There was no storm radar or weather forecasting in the 1940s, and we flew blindly into a dangerously violent thunderstorm over the mountains south of Pittsburgh. The plane pitched, plummeted, and bumped violently up and down. The copilot and I struggled to keep control. One bump was so severe that a passenger came flying into the cockpit so forcibly that he was wedged under the control pedestal. The impact broke his leg. Several other passengers suffered fairly serious head injuries.

We finally flew out of the storm, but many of the passengers needed immediate medical attention. The closest hospital was in Pittsburgh, behind us. Steeling myself to fly through the storm a second time, I turned the plane around. Fortunately, the storm had passed. In Pittsburgh four passengers were taken by waiting ambulances to the hospital. As a consequence of our emergency return to Pittsburgh, we didn't reach our base until early the next morning. That flight made a lasting impression. I always, to this day, wear a seat belt when I'm on a plane.

On December 10, my group moved to Fort Wayne, Indiana. Each crew received a brand new C-47. We were informed that we would soon depart for England. We began our preparations to go.

Leaving Flavil was the most difficult part of my preparations. Our honeymoon had extended from Altus to Austin and included our time in Nebraska, North Carolina, and Indiana. Flavil had traveled by bus to each base. Now, very much in love, we hoped we would survive the difficulties ahead and meet again. We said goodbye on Christmas Eve, 1943. I left Fort Wayne to begin the long flight to England.

Flavil's ensuing life as the wife of an overseas pilot took its own exciting turn. She returned to Jacksonville to start a nursery school for working mothers. Eight months later, she moved to Greenwich Village. Her roommate, a member of Martha Graham's dance troupe, introduced Flavil to some of the exciting culture of New York.

Flavil found a job running a kindergarten in Harlem where she met Evelyn Necarsulmar, who worked for New York City supervising the quality of kindergartens. Evelyn, a wealthy single woman, had adopted a son and daughter who were nine and ten years old. Evelyn was impressed with Flavil and her skills, and invited her to move into her Park Avenue apartment. In return, Flavil watched Evelyn's children before and after school. Evelyn also found Flavil a job at Ethical Culture, the innovative, progressive school her children attended. Flavil became an indelible part of their family, spending summertime with them at their vacation home in Connecticut.

Flavil also met and enjoyed Evelyn's friends and neighbors. One, Dr. Benjamin Spock, was in the process of writing a book titled *Baby and Child Care*. Flavil had studied child psychology at the University of Tennessee, and Dr. Spock asked her to proofread one of his chapters. It was testament to what a bright and creative person she was. Of course we now know Dr. Spock's book sold millions of copies, becoming the "bible" of child rearing after the war. At the time, her association with Spock and numerous other fascinating people in New York was always cause for excitement in my receiving another letter from her while I was on the other side of the Atlantic.

V

War over Europe

Leaving Fort Wayne on Christmas Eve, 1943, we flew to Morrison Field in West Palm Beach, Florida, to begin our journey to England. Our planes, however, lacked the range to fly directly to England. We followed the 9,700-mile South Atlantic Air Ferry Route. This meant flying from Florida to Brazil, across the Atlantic to the west coast of Africa, then north to England. The shorter route through Greenland wasn't used because too many planes had crashed because of bad weather over the North Atlantic.

On Christmas Day, we left West Palm Beach and flew to Borinquen Field, Puerto Rico. Woody came down with a bad cold, which grounded us for three days. When he was better, we flew to Georgetown, British Guyana, south of Venezuela. On the next leg to Natal, Brazil, we crossed over the mouth of the Amazon. It was bigger than I ever could have imagined. We flew above it for almost thirty minutes and could see its muddy waters extending out into the ocean beyond our vision.

Natal sits at the tip of a peninsula that offers the shortest distance across the Atlantic. The leg to Ascension Island, our stop in the middle of the Atlantic, was 1,400 miles, the outer limit of our C-47s' range. Eight fuel tanks, like barrels in a row, were installed in the passenger cabin to increase capacity. We squeezed every last cup of fuel possible into the tanks, turning us essentially into a flying bomb. Each plane had a crew of five plus eight passengers, all of them glider pilots. Unfortunately, smoking was common in those days. Before takeoff, I made it clear to the passengers that if any one of them even thought about lighting a cigarette, I would throw them out of the plane. I was quite concerned, since I thought all glider pilots were nutty.

On New Year's Eve, we took off a little after 9:00 p.m. Our maintenance officer had squirreled parts and supplies for the aircraft into every nook and cranny. With passengers, spare parts, and fuel, we weighed over 32,000 pounds, far exceeding the manufacturer's maximum takeoff weight of 25,900 pounds. The runway ended at the ocean. We roared forward—fortunately lifting off before reaching the water. But it took us an hour to climb to nine thousand feet, something that normally would take fifteen minutes.

We were part of a constant stream of planes crossing the Atlantic. Natal had one plane taking off every ten minutes around the clock. I was flying as Woody slept, still trying to recover from his cold. It was a clear night. The navigator had given me a compass heading, which I was following when I happened to see a red light ahead. I figured it must be the red light on the left wing of the forward plane, so I fell in to follow it. In a few minutes the navigator burst into the cockpit.

"Where the hell are you going?" he demanded.

"I'm just following the plane ahead of us," I said.

"You stupid bastard, that's not a plane. That's Mars! Get back on course!"

Without debate, I did.

We found Ascension Island sitting in the middle of the Atlantic, a welcome sight indeed. Early in the morning we made the relatively short flight to Roberts Field in Liberia on the coast of Africa. On the next leg, we went to Rufisque, Senegal, across the bay from Dakar. We landed on a runway made of Marsden matting, interlocking sections of perforated steel planking that could be laid down almost anywhere on relatively even ground to create a landing strip.

While we were in the operations office the next morning, signing out for departure, a B-24 bomber outside started down the runway. B-24s had tricycle landing gears, with a wheel under the nose. Hearing the roar of a plane taking off, we looked out at the field. The plane was going 50 or 60 miles an hour when its nose wheel hit something, probably a depression in the Marsden matting. The wheel collapsed. The plane hit the ground. The fuel tanks in the wings ruptured, spilling fuel onto the engines.

The plane exploded. All seven men on board died instantly.

This somber experience, and the awareness that any of us might not see home again, occupied our thoughts and conversations for days.

We hit a bad storm on the way to our next stop in Marrakech, Morocco. Because the weather was so bad, and so many planes were already grounded in Marrakech, we were one of the last planes allowed to land before the airfield closed because of overcrowding. The only available quarters for us were tents sandwiched between trees in an olive grove. They didn't provide much protection—1,500 feet up in the Atlas Mountains—from the bitterly cold January nights. We crawled into our sleeping bags wearing our full winter flying uniforms, including boots, hoping to stay warm.

After ten days stuck in Marrakech, we finally took off on the last leg to Newquay, England. We had to fly well out over the Atlantic, away from Portugal and Spain, to avoid the Germans. Once over the Atlantic, we ran into another severe storm.

It was so wet and cold that our wings started icing immediately. Ice on airplane wings interferes with the airflow over the top of the wing surface that creates the lift necessary to make a plane fly. Without proper lift, a plane will lose altitude and crash. The only solution was to de-ice the wings.

De-icing was an elementary process in those days. An inflatable rubber boot spanned the front of the wing. It could be expanded with air pressure, like a balloon, to break up ice and force it off the wing. The process was tricky. You had to wait until the ice was solid enough to break when you inflated the boot, but not wait too long or the wing lost lift. If you inflated the boot too soon, the ice would flex and freeze in the shape of the expanded boot. If that happened, you couldn't break the ice away, and you were in serious trouble.

Ice coated our wings as we flew. As our lift diminished, we would lose elevation while waiting for sufficient ice to accumulate for the de-icing boot to work. After inflating the boot and breaking the ice, we'd get back on track, gaining elevation until the next accumulation of ice took us back down again.

Several times we became so bogged down with ice that we flew a mere hundred feet above the Atlantic, hoping the ocean air would be warm enough to melt the ice. It wasn't. And the visibility was so bad, we were afraid we might fly into a ship before we could see it.

We felt an enormous sense of relief when we saw the green southern tip of Ireland. That meant we were only forty minutes away from Newquay. We landed after twelve hours and twenty minutes of very exhausting flying. We checked into operations, stretched our legs, refueled, and continued on to our new base at Bottesford, in the middle of England, seventeen miles northeast of Nottingham. Late on the night of January 15, 1944, we finally reached our destination.

We became part of the Allied Airborne Army, commanded by Lieutenant General Louis Brereton. Our routine for the next two months was the same as we'd had in North Carolina, flying formations and towing gliders.

Two months later, the 436th transferred to Membury Airfield, about fifty miles west of London. There were several other air bases in the area for troop carrier units, and a base for parachute airborne divisions. At Membury, each of our four squadrons was increased from eighteen to twenty-five planes. I was made pilot of my own plane, serial number 2100562. Its call sign was Wishwell-Easy. Wishwell was the designation for all planes in the 82nd squadron and Easy stood for *E*. It was a great plane and remained my plane until I came home a year and a half later.

Late one afternoon, I was in my barracks and heard a plane take off—and then the horrible sound of it crashing. I ran out to see a C-47 on fire about a hundred yards away. Bodies were scattered, some on fire. I grabbed a fire extinguisher and ran to the crash site. It was so hot, I couldn't get close. There was nothing I or anyone could do. All the passengers and crew were killed. It was another reminder of how vulnerable we were.

Despite such tragedies, there were humorous moments as well. We continued to train pulling gliders. One of the pilots, Charlie Hastings, was towing a glider one day and thought it would be fun to see what would happen to the folks in the glider if he did a slow roll with the tow plane. On landing, he approached the glider, eager to enjoy the results of his prank, only to discover that the colonel, our commanding officer, had been in the glider. He was as mad as a wet cat. The colonel did not appreciate Charlie's reasoning that every glider pilot needed to be trained to deal with unexpected flight challenges.

We also conducted glider-towing practice at night, which was grim. It is difficult to navigate a glider at night. There were many crashes. One of the glider pilots missed the runway on landing and managed to destroy six gliders parked beside the runway. He was celebrated on our base as the first "reverse glider ace" of the war. The higher-ups suddenly decided night glider flights were too costly and canceled them (and moved parked gliders farther from the runways).

Our leaders at the First Allied Army Headquarters in Croydon, near London, believed that their access to fresh eggs was essential to the war effort. Every week, headquarters ordered two planes to Belfast to pick up eggs. A crate was put on each plane to guarantee delivery. I was dispatched on the egg run once. I arrived in Belfast in the afternoon. After checking in, my copilot and I went to the officers' club and started drinking Irish whiskey, much earlier than prudent. I'd never had Irish whiskey before, and my enjoyment masked any awareness of its potency. That evening, when I stepped outside the club, the impact of the cold night air and the whiskey froze me in my tracks. I stood paralyzed. Fortunately, a flight nurse who'd been inside with us took me by the arm and guided me safely back to the officers' quarters.

I awoke the next morning feeling fine and delivered the eggs to Croydon. When we were waiting on the taxiway for takeoff for Membury, a four-engine British bomber landed short of the runway. It touched down in a turnip field that had been planted around the airfield in an effort to use every inch of ground to grow much-needed food. Turnips and greens, churned up and finely chopped by the propellers, went flying through the air—a very funny sight. Although the turnips were lost, the crew and plane survived.

My life on the base at Membury was fairly pleasant. When I wasn't on duty, I liked to read, especially European history. I also spent time with friends. My closest friends were Doc Mack, J. J. Lawson, and Charlie Butler. Doc, from California, was our flight surgeon. J. J., from South Boston, Virginia, was our assistant operations officer. Charlie, a brilliant mechanic and the squadron maintenance officer, was an absolute tyrant about every detail. I was confident that my plane was always in excellent condition.

The army took care of most of our needs. We were well fed. Our laundry was done, and there was a communal shower that we were authorized to use once a week. I didn't need to buy much other than shaving cream and toothpaste, so I sent most of my pay home to Flavil. There was a pleasant old pub, The Hare and The Hound, on the base just down the road from my barracks. But since I didn't smoke or drink much, I didn't spend much time or money there.

Occasionally when I was given leave, I would take the train an hour into London to go sightseeing. I liked to visit art museums, walk in the parks, and wander through the city, seeing places I'd read about.

At some point in my tenure at Membury, a wooden glider box came to be parked near our barracks. Forty feet long, ten feet wide, and eight feet high, it was big enough for some of us to turn it into a cozy home. Seven pilots, some of them glider pilots, and I moved our cots and footlockers in and set up house. We cut out windows, added shutters, and installed a coal stove with a stovepipe sticking out the top. We ate in the mess hall, but we were able to cook simple things like eggs, which local farmers were happy to trade for cigarettes. It was a grand place.

Most of our time before June 1944 was spent training and flying. We flew formations, sometimes as a squadron, sometimes as a group, and sometimes with several groups in a line. One night we performed a massive exercise. The entire troop carrier command was in the air. We were practicing for something big.

We knew it would be the invasion of France, but we didn't know where or when.

In early June we got orders that no one was to leave the base. We knew something was brewing. The morning of June 5, a briefing was called for all flight crews. There were two hundred or so of us in the theater. The colonel told us that the invasion of France would start that evening. Our task was to drop paratroopers behind the beaches of Normandy, just after midnight. Our mood was subdued and serious as we received our missions. My task was to drop twenty-one paratroopers from the 501st Battalion of the 82nd Airborne, near the town of Sainte-Mère-Église.

We were given an intelligence briefing that the Allies had air superiority in the area so there should be no concern about German fighter planes. We would be flying so low that any anti-aircraft guns still in operation should not be effective against us. Undoubtedly we would run into ground fire, mostly small-arms fire, which could still bring down a plane by hitting a fuel tank or vital crew member. Many of us had metal under our seats that we hoped was some protection from ground fire.

Crews spent the day getting the planes ready. We painted three broad white stripes under each wing so the US Navy could recognize us. The previous summer, the navy had mistakenly shot down twenty-three American planes during the invasion of Italy.

Men polished their boots and wrote letters home. My friend Charlie Hastings put together a little wicker basket with toilet paper, a box of cigars, and a can of chocolate to take with him in the event he was shot down and captured. He was a bit of a nut.

About 9:00 p.m., I sat in the cockpit of my plane as twenty-one paratroopers, each carrying seventy pounds of equipment plus their parachutes, boarded my plane. We taxied onto the runway. Wings staggered, we squeezed the planes as close together as possible. We waited. An ambulance came screeching to the front of the line of planes. Our squadron leader, Major Bernie White-house, had had a heart attack while waiting to take off for D-Day. He was carried out on a stretcher. This did not do a hell of a lot for the morale of the pilots of the 82nd.

As we waited for the operations officer to replace the major, there was still enough light in the June sky to see it fill with planes. It was very orderly. The 434th, 435th, 437th, and 438th took off and flew in great circles around the airfields where we were based, waiting for other squadrons to fall in line. It was a spectacular sight: hundreds and hundreds of planes flying in formation, reflecting the rays of the setting sun. The 436th was last, maybe because of the major's heart attack. I was in the last five-plane element of the last squadron of my group. A few other groups fell in behind us.

It grew dark, and we headed east toward France. As we approached the channel, I caught sight of thousands of ships under way for the Normandy coast. I'd never seen so many ships. Apparently 5,000 ships and 1,300 planes transported about 160,000 troops across the English Channel that night and into the morning of June 6.

We were several miles south of the German-occupied island of Alderney when suddenly I saw beautiful, glowing, orange balls shooting into the air like fireworks. I thought, "This is really pretty." That thought quickly changed to, "My God, those sons of bitches are shooting at us!" Fortunately, our intelligence was good. We were out of range. Those beautiful "fireworks" were my first encounter with enemy fire.

We flew exactly as we'd trained, in five-plane, V-shaped elements, each element flying a little higher than the element in front to avoid their prop wash, which can make flying rough. I was the left rear plane, with my right propeller no more than five feet from the left wing of the plane ahead of mine. With no room for error, I had to keep one hand on the throttle and one on the wheel, making constant, minute adjustments. If you let your guard down for a second, you could get into real trouble fast. We flew without lights, so the faint glow of the engine exhaust of the plane in front served as our guiding light.

When we got to the Cotentin Peninsula of Normandy, we turned north. We were met with sporadic ground fire, but fortunately no anti-aircraft fire. As we approached the drop zone, I turned on the orange "ready" light in back, signaling the paratroopers to hook up and prepare to jump. At this point we were listening for a radio signal or looking for a ground beacon from a pathfinder stick, placed by the 9th Pathfinder Group, which had parachuted in ahead of the main force. This signal would identify the precise drop zone.

We immediately picked up the signal and realized that we had arrived at the drop zone sooner than expected. There was a stronger tailwind over the peninsula than predicted, which meant that by the time the last of our guys jumped, they'd end up in the English Channel. Loaded down as they were, they would sink like rocks. I decided to take a risk.

Flying on the left wing of the last element of the 82nd, which was the last of the 436th group, I knew I had about five minutes before the next group of planes was scheduled to arrive over the jump zone. I made a very steep left turn and came back around to give the troops a chance to land near the drop zone. Close to the designated drop zone, I hit the green jump light. I hope I gave them the chance to land safely where intended. We were at four hundred feet, which allows the paratrooper time for one swing in a parachute before hitting the ground. As soon as the last guy jumped, we pulled up and got the hell out of there.

I heard later that the paratroopers dropped around Sainte-Mère-Église suffered heavy casualties. Some drowned in fields flooded by the Germans. Others were shot while still in the air. Some became sitting ducks, stuck in trees or hung up on wires. Many of those who did hit the ground were unable to find their squadrons. They were, however, creative, brave, and persistent. By 5:00 a.m., June 6, Sainte-Mère-Église was the first town in France liberated from the Germans.

There had been no training for the flight back. There were no formations. Every plane found its own way home as fast as it could. We did form small groups with other planes we recognized. We looked for a landmark on the English side of the channel, a runway brightly lit by big bonfires. This was the beacon fire the RAF maintained to help damaged planes find the nearest safe runway. Every pilot knew that if he made it that far, there would be a place to land.

We spotted the bonfire, but since we weren't damaged, we got our bearings and headed for Membury. Landing about 2:30 a.m., we taxied to our revetment and turned off our engines. The copilot and I just sat in our seats, totally exhausted. A medic arrived and gave each member of the crew a big shot of Old Overholt rye whiskey. I don't know whether that was helpful or not, but we all took it.

The next day we awoke to find several empty beds in the barracks. It turned out those flyers had been shot down the night before and were all dead, and sadly, my dear friend Woody was one of them. In a somber mood, we went to our briefing. We were to tow gliders late that afternoon to a landing zone close to the previous night's drop zone.

Flying over the English Channel on the afternoon of June 6—D-Day—we saw the huge armada in daylight. There were so many ships, it looked like a person could walk across the channel by stepping from one to the next.

We became aware of a major problem once we were over France. The designated landing zone was still in German hands.

And we did not have enough fuel to tow the gliders back to England.

We had to cut them loose. That part of the Cotentin Peninsula was mostly farmland, with many small fields bordered by hedgerows. The hedgerows, many of which dated from Roman times, were berms of rock and soil, three to five feet tall and just as wide, covered with mature hedges and small trees. The hedgerows were deadly for gliders. Looking down, we could see gliders that had crashed into them. We couldn't see a straightaway long enough for a glider to land safely. Our return to Membury was without joy. The glider pilots we had cut loose were dear friends.

That night the barracks felt empty and eerie. More pilots had been shot down, and most of the glider pilots were gone. I tried to fall asleep, but couldn't. I thought of lost friends, crashed gliders, and the poor men on the ground. A nearby pilot's crying and moaning kept me awake. He was having a nightmare.

"Please be quiet," I said, trying to wake him.

He kept moaning. I got up, walked over, and shook him. He still didn't wake up. So I slapped him. To this day I remain deeply ashamed for doing that, but at the time, I was desperate for sleep. I needed him to stop.

Over the next few days, I made several more flights to France to drop supplies, either on the beachhead or just beyond. When the Germans were pushed back far enough, we landed on makeshift runways. Some were so short, we had to cut power as soon as our wheels touched the ground—something you normally shouldn't do. Our ground troops, bombers, and fighter pilots had all done their jobs, so we were free from enemy fire, making flying a lot safer. Eventually, once more supplies arrived by ship, there was less pressure on troop carrier planes to fly as many supply missions. We were sent on leave for rest and relaxation, a few crews at a time.

My crew was sent to Torquay, a resort city on the southern coast of England, where the US military had taken over a few hotels. I got to do whatever I wanted for a few days. I rode horses, played miniature golf, enjoyed the shore, and sat reading on the hotel porch. It was a very pleasant change of pace.

VI

Italy, Southern France, and Market Garden

When I got back from Torquay, I discovered that about two-thirds of the 436th had been assigned to take part in the invasion of southern France, otherwise known as Operation Dragoon. They were being sent to a base fifty miles northeast of Rome on the Italian coast. I was not interested in more action, but Italy is rich in history. The idea of seeing it appealed to me. Fortuitously, one of my friends, a copilot, didn't want to go, so I volunteered in his place.

We took off at night and flew due south over the Atlantic, again putting a wide buffer between us and Spain and Portugal. We flew across the northern part of Morocco to Rabat, where we refueled and rested before flying across the Mediterranean Sea to our base, just north of the ancient Roman port of Civitavecchia. The dirt runway, merely a big wheat field bulldozed flat, was next to the beach. The beach and the land near it were riddled for miles with German land mines. Local residents had marked a safe path through the mines to the beach. Nobody deviated from that path. My pilot and I were assigned a two-man tent that sat, with several other tents, in a hollow between the minefield and the runway.

We were one of about a hundred planes. We spent several weeks doing routine formation exercises and flying occasional errands. I was assigned as lead pilot of a group of planes flying enlisted men over the Italian boot to Foggia. It was on the eastern coast of Italy, whereas Civitavecchia was on the western coast. Between the two were the Apennine Mountains, a significant mountain range, with elevations up to 9,500 feet. Our route involved going through a pass in the mountains. Unfortunately, our navigator identified the wrong area as the entrance to the pass. As the valley became narrower, the sides steeper, it was obvious that we were not in any kind of a pass. Where we were was . . . in a very difficult situation.

There wasn't room to turn around, or time to throw things out to lighten the plane. I used full power to push the plane as high as I could, and told the radio operator to warn the planes behind us to turn back. With no voice radio contact, my radio operator sent a Morse code message for the others to turn around immediately. They did.

The mountain was rising toward us more quickly than our plane was gaining altitude. I could see the summit ahead and wasn't sure we could get above it. With my wings almost touching the cliffs on either side, we squeezed through the narrow cleft. I think we nearly bounced off the top of the ridge, but we made it!

A few nights later, we had a night flying exercise. The weather had been very dry. After the first few planes landed, the runway was obscured by a heavy curtain of dust. Visibility with the dark and the dust was near zero. We landed safely, but before we could get off the runway, another plane landed and taxied into us, its left propeller shredding our right wing. Sitting in the copilot seat on the right side of our plane gave me a better view of the damage than I cared to have. Fortunately, our fuel tanks weren't hit. Amazingly, no one was hurt in what could have been a major tragedy. Both crews, with various bottles of alcohol in hand, wove through the minefield to the beach to soothe shattered nerves. While I drank, I pondered the wisdom of volunteering.

A heavy rain came a few nights later to dampen the dust. I woke in the morning to see my shoes floating nearly at the level of my face. Our little hollow had become a pond. Water had risen up to my cot.

I enjoyed my time in the Civitavecchia area. There was a lot to do during my downtime. If I wasn't relaxing or swimming at the beach, I was visiting historical sites. Civitavecchia is an ancient Roman port. I saw the remains of the old town walls, medieval piazzas, and a sixteenth-century fortification called Forte Michelangelo. Wandering around, I stumbled upon an abandoned German grenade factory, where I tucked away a harmless grenade as a souvenir. I also visited Rome, just fifty miles to the southwest. I soaked in the history there, including the Coliseum, the Parthenon, Saint Peter's Basilica, and a portion of the old Apian Way.

I knew quite a lot about Roman history, so it was the everyday Italian things that took me most by surprise. I discovered pizza. But the most exciting thing was my first encounter with an espresso machine, hissing and erupting with steam like a small Vesuvius. I also encountered some toilets that might have been used by the ancient Romans.

August 15 was the beginning of the invasion of southern France. It was a similar operation to D-Day. Ground forces came ashore between Toulon and Cannes, while paratroopers and gliders were dropped inland. It was a beautiful summer day. My mission was to carry paratroopers and tow a glider to a landing zone near Marseille. As we lined up on the runway, an officer from group headquarters came aboard and took my seat as copilot. This was his prerogative, but as I moved into the back, I felt like a useless fool.

I was heading into an invasion with nothing to do but sit and look out the window. Over the Mediterranean, one of the gliders, towed by another plane in our group, lost a wing. It spun out of control. The pilot of the tow plane had no choice but to cut it loose. We watched it plummet into the sea. With no parachutes, the poor men on board didn't have a chance.

Unlike D-Day, not a shot was fired at any of our aircraft during this invasion. The Germans had abandoned the area before we arrived. In fact, the entire invasion met with little resistance.

My group was ordered back to Membury in late August. We stopped in Gibraltar to refuel. The Rock of Gibraltar sits at the mouth of the Strait of Gibraltar, which connects the Mediterranean to the Atlantic. The runway, built out into the water, extended beyond both sides of the Rock. There was usually a strong crosswind. To land in a crosswind I had to crab the plane into the wind, which means pointing the nose of the plane more into the wind than toward the runway so that the wind doesn't blow the plane off to the side. Just before the wheels hit the runway, I then had to quickly point the nose straight down the runway. On our approach, as expected, a strong crosswind hit us. It didn't help my confidence to see the tails of airplanes sticking out of the water on either side of the runway. I crabbed into the wind. When the plane went behind the Rock of Gibraltar, which blocked the wind, I turned straight to the runway. Suddenly I had to crab again when the wind slammed into us as we cleared the Rock. I was either good enough or lucky enough to maintain control. We landed safely. It was depressing, however, to see yet another plane sticking out of the water nearby.

I returned safely to Membury, my eagerness to volunteer significantly reduced. We began almost immediately preparing for Operation Market Garden, which was British Field Marshal Bernard Montgomery's plan to end the war by Christmas. The objective was to drop paratroopers into Holland, and seize and hold the towns and bridges on a key north–south highway. If it was successful, ground troops and supplies could then move rapidly into Germany from the north.

Market Garden began on September 17 and was the largest airborne operation to that point in the war. The day was bright and sunny. We took off with twenty-one British paratroopers. Our drop zone was the Phillips Electric Company factory in Eindhoven, Holland. Flying in broad daylight over enemy territory, we were met with hostile fire from both anti-aircraft guns and ground fire. A number of our planes were shot down. Brave Dutch citizens rushed to save and hide as many of our pilots as possible. One of our pilots, Guido Brasseco, broke his leg when he crashed. Fortunately, he was quickly rescued. With a wig placed on his head, and dressed as a woman, he was hidden in the women's birthing ward of a hospital while his leg healed. Many other downed pilots were helped to escape to freedom in Scandinavia.

Our mission the next day was to tow two gliders to a landing zone in the same area. We towed them in what's called an echelon formation, where you fly in groups of four, each plane to the right of and slightly behind the forward plane, about half a mile apart. There was the lead ship, the second ship, and on down the line. I was flying the lead ship of my echelon.

We were about ten miles from the landing zone when anti-aircraft fire started. The lead ship of the echelon in front of me was shot down. We were close enough that I could see the guns firing from a churchyard below to our left. Since we had two gliders in tow, there was no possibility of taking evasive action. We watched as the planes of the echelon in front of us were methodically shot down like sitting ducks. My copilot, Bernie Lang, and I made eye contact, then looked away. We knew we were next and could do nothing but wait for the end. Neither of us spoke.

Just then, two RAF Spitfires blew past us and destroyed the churchyard gun emplacement. The relief and joy we felt in that moment is beyond words. Not surprisingly, I have a high regard and a deep affection for the Royal Air Force to this day.

Though that was a harrowing experience, the next day held one of the most frightening experiences of my life. Our crew was preparing to tow another glider to Holland when Major Rowerdink from group headquarters came up and told my copilot to give him the copilot seat for the flight. It was the prerogative of officers from group headquarters to do this whenever they chose. I knew the major by name only. We said little to each other on takeoff.

Over the channel, the weather changed. The surface of the channel was as still and unruffled as a millpond. The sky and water, the same color of gray, merged together. There was no visible horizon. I was flying into a big gray wall. Suddenly I was seized by an extremely bad case of vertigo. Every sensation in my body told me that we were in a vertical left bank. I was convinced that our left wingtip was pointing straight down to the sea. The feeling was so intense that I thought we were going to crash. I yelled over to Major Rowerdink, "Take the controls. I have vertigo!"

"You're doing a great job, Boyd," he replied calmly.

It's the responsibility of a copilot to take the controls when the pilot commands. Instead, Major Rowerdink folded his arms across his chest and refused to touch the controls. I struggled for what was probably ten minutes but seemed like forever. I felt I was having a nervous breakdown. I kept telling myself that I had to look at the instruments and fly by what they said—not by what I felt. I relied on the compass needle, the gyroscopic ball, and the air speed indicator. All confirmed we were flying straight and level. I knew that if I responded to my instincts while towing a glider, I would kill us all. Just as the vertigo started to leave me, the mission was canceled because of the bad weather. Unfortunately, that wasn't my last encounter with Major Rowerdink.

The most northerly point of Operation Market Garden was Arnhem, fifty miles from Eindhoven. The British 1st Airborne Division dropped more than ten thousand men into the Arnhem area by parachute and glider from September 17 to September 19.

The plan was that ground troops under the command of Field Marshal Montgomery would push north from France and reach the airborne units by September 22 with the necessary support and supplies to hold the road. The 1st Airborne expected limited resistance from what was thought to be a reserve German force in the area. Because of poor intelligence, they landed almost on top of two full German divisions and two panzer divisions. They were surrounded and under heavy attack.

With the 1st Airborne troops fighting for their lives, we were making as many trips as possible across the channel. We took supplies from RAF airfields in England to drop on the positions the troops held. Bad weather soon set in and prevented resupply trips for many days. When weather permitted, we pushed hard to continue our resupply flights. The distance was relatively short, so with luck, we could make four trips. Late one afternoon, aware that the airborne troops were in a deadly situation, we picked up a fifth load before dark. We taxied up to a warehouse on an RAF base about four in the afternoon. As we approached, however, the loading crew walked away. I yelled to the British sergeant that we were ready for another load for the 1st Airborne.

"F-you, you Yank. We're going to have our tea. *Then* we'll load your f-ing plane."

I was shocked. Some things are deeply ingrained—and tea-time in Britain is apparently one of them. We sat and waited. It seemed to me—and it was widely believed by others—that Field Marshal Montgomery, like that loading crew, took too much time responding with help for the 1st Airborne.

Left by themselves in a hopeless situation, the 1st was over-run. Market Garden was a failure. Hope of ending the war by Christmas was lost.

VII

France

Fall 1944 was spent flying supply missions to various elements of the army as well as evacuating wounded troops. We would land and take off on makeshift airfields near the army field hospitals and fly the wounded back to airfields in England. These field hospitals constantly moved forward to stay near the fighting. We had space for twenty-one stretchers on the plane. The soldiers we carried were seriously wounded, yet they were the happiest guys I ever saw. They knew that for them, the war was over. Two nurses accompanied us on those flights, and without exception, they were marvelous, loving, tender, and extremely competent.

During that time I had some delightful encounters with RAF pilots—in addition to the time they saved my life. One night we were flying in weather so bad that I decided it was too dangerous to return to our base. We sighted an RAF airfield and radioed Membury that we'd be spending the night there. I knew that we could land at any US or RAF air base and be welcomed as one of their own.

I dropped my bag in my quarters and went to the officers' club. I knew I would find instant camaraderie and some very interesting characters. I fell in with a couple of RAF pilots who flew mosquitoes—very fast, light, low-level bombers. They said they were going to France to drop a load that night and welcomed me to come along. I thought about my experience volunteering in Italy and said thanks, but no thanks. They understood. Once in an officers' club at another RAF base, I saw footprints that wandered all the way across the ceiling. Clearly, RAF pilots were good flyers—and excelled at having fun.

In early December, we learned the 436th was moving to France just after the New Year. The destined base was near the small city of Melun, on the Seine River, about thirty-five miles southeast of Paris. The airfield was being vacated by a Douglas A-20 attack bomber group that was relocating closer to Germany. I was sent as part of a small advance party to check out the runway and other facilities.

We arrived at the officers' club for dinner that evening and discovered our hosts were attempting to drink all the alcohol at the bar. Their logic was that drinking the liquor was easier than moving the bottles to the new base. Asked to help, we lent our enthusiastic support. They introduced us to the French 75, a concoction named for the main French artillery gun of World War I. It was indeed lethal, consisting of one-quarter cognac and three-quarters champagne. I have no idea how many I drank. I remember feeling like I had been shot out of a gun as I walked home later, my feet never touching the ground.

On December 16, 1944, the Germans launched a major offensive, one that became infamously known as the Battle of the Bulge, the largest and bloodiest battle the United States fought during the war. It started with a surprise attack on the American garrisons around Bastogne, Belgium. Within a few days the 101st Airborne arrived as reinforcements. By December 21, Bastogne and the 101st were surrounded. A German emissary arrived to demand their surrender. General Anthony McAuliffe, commander of the 101st, blurted a four-letter profanity that was softened to the famous four-letter response he sent to the Germans. "Nuts."

It infuriated the Germans—but inspired us.

Bastogne was like Operation Market Garden all over again. We were desperate to ensure that our infantry and the 101st Airborne didn't meet the fate of the 1st British Airborne. Our missions were limited, however, by the heavy anti-aircraft fire and German fighter planes. We couldn't make a drop without RAF fighter planes flying low cover for us, shooting anything that moved.

I made several drops around Bastogne. Sometimes the weather was clear enough that I could see the poor guys on the ground. What a miserable-looking group they were, stuck in the bitter cold, with snow everywhere and no place to go but a foxhole or, if they were lucky, a tent. Some of them had been deployed without proper winter coats or boots—this during one of the coldest winters on record. I felt deeply sorry for them, but I was glad I'd become a pilot. I became newly appreciative of returning to base and my warm bed every night.

On Christmas Eve the weather worsened. Fog moved in, grounding us for two days. By the time we could restart our supply drops, General George Patton's Third Army had punched through enemy lines and reached Bastogne, ending the siege. General Patton moved much faster than Field Marshal Montgomery—no doubt forgoing any interludes for tea.

Our experience of winter hardship that cold, snowy December was augmented by someone putting soap flakes in the camp food. At least that was the assumption, since an ensuing investigation discovered neither cause nor culprit. However, every person who ate in the mess hall one very cold evening awoke in the night and went dashing through the snow for the latrines. Hundreds of desperate men fled in agony, searching for a bathroom or a bush. One man broke his leg in the rush. Those of us living in the glider box appreciated its proximity to the latrines. We didn't have as far to trot.

As planned, shortly after New Year's Day, the 436th moved to Melun. Our accommodations were rough, with six-man tents, outdoor latrines, and primitive bathing facilities. Still, no one complained. There was heavy snow, and temperatures were in the teens, but at least we weren't on the front lines. Everyone felt for those guys, especially those in the north, where the Battle of the Bulge raged for another two weeks.

I had neither the inclination nor the time to think much about life after the war until we won the Battle of the Bulge. Until that victory, I just focused on what was in front of me that needed to be done. After the Battle of the Bulge, I began to believe that I might get to go home alive. We began to talk about what we were going to do after the fighting ceased. Doc Mack knew that he'd still be a doctor. J. J. would go back to buying tobacco for Lucky Strike cigarettes. And Charlie couldn't help but be a mechanic. I was the youngest and the only one without a plan.

J. J., his rich southern Virginia accent as thick as gravy, said, "My brother, Robert, is a partner in a big law firm in West Virginia. And he's making a lot of money. He went to law school at the University of Virginia in Charlottesville. You ought to go there, too."

With some excitement, I wrote Flavil that after the war, we'd be going to Charlottesville—wherever that was—so I could attend law school.

In January and for several months afterward, we did a lot of flying, delivering supplies and transporting the wounded. By March, the ground troops were approaching Germany. The Rhine River acted as a natural barrier against the Allied advance. The Germans blew up bridges as they retreated across them, effectively halting the Allies.

A break came on March 7, when the Ludendorff Bridge in the town of Remagen was captured—mostly intact. It provided the Allies their first bridge access beyond the Rhine. Fighting for control of the bridge had been fierce. My crew and I were sent to pick up the wounded. The Germans continued to launch a fierce artillery attack on the western end of the bridge, one so intense that it became known as Dead Man's Corner. I landed in a tree-lined pasture that sat on a bluff overlooking the bridge. My focus, however, was on the twenty-one soldiers who desperately needed transport to a hospital, each suffering from severe head wounds. The crew and I helped load the plane.

As we began our liftoff, I could see that we weren't going to clear the trees at the end of the field. If I tried to climb at a steeper angle, the plane would stall and crash, probably killing everyone on board. Our only chance was to fly into—and ideally through—the trees. We hit the treetops—and plowed through into the air.

I was jubilant, thinking we were set for the flight back. But soon I noticed that my right engine was beginning to overheat. I shut it down—and flew on one engine.

About twenty minutes later, I spotted an airfield with Spit-fires, so I knew it was an RAF base. We touched down, and, as I knew would happen, the Brits took excellent care of us. The wounded were tended to, the crew and I were served tea, and the engine was repaired. The cause of the overheating was a tree limb that had gotten jammed in the air scoop, blocking the cooling mechanism. The mechanics fixed it and got us back on our way. My appreciation for the RAF mounted further.

One of the pleasures of my stay in Melun was being able to hop a supply truck to Paris whenever I had leave. I would get dropped off at the Place de la Concorde at one end of the Champs-Élysees and spend the day exploring the city. Paris had a wonderful subway system laid out like the spokes of a wheel. I decided to go out to the end of the line of each spoke and walk back to the center of town. It was interesting to take in the different neighborhoods, from the poor working-class ones to the sophisticated ones. I was a fast walker, but when something caught my interest, I stopped to explore. I would buy bread at the boulangeries and eat lunch in small cafés. The meals were always good. I would arrive back at the Place de la Concorde in the late afternoon in time to catch the supply truck back to the base. These walks gave me a deep affection for the city I still love.

My very first visit into Paris was in August 1944, just two days after its liberation from the Germans. We landed at Le Bourget, the Paris airport, to deliver a load of blood plasma. Our orders were to return immediately to England, but the crew and I decided we should spend the night. It was a wonderful, wild, and happy night. We were not allowed to pay for anything anywhere. No bar, café, or restaurant would accept our money. There was constant celebration and drinking. Fortunately, late that night, a very kind French couple helped me find my hotel.

During my explorations of Paris, I learned that the Red Cross gave tickets to servicemen to attend theater performances. When

I checked, I was asked if I liked opera. Of course! Whereupon I was handed a ticket for a performance that evening. The Paris Opera House, known as the Palais Garnier, was completed in 1875. Stunningly ornate, it is considered one of Paris's outstanding landmarks.

For my first experience of live opera, I sat alone in the president's box, just left of the stage, in the most beautiful opera house in the world. There was not a better seat or a more satisfied opera patron in the place. The opera was *Faust*. The voice of the bass who sang the role of Mephistopheles was so deep and resonant that it thrilled my soul. I had come a long way from listening to the Metropolitan Opera radio broadcasts in Macclenny with Mother.

On March 22, two weeks after the bridge at Remagen was captured, General Patton's troops crossed the Rhine farther south and pushed rapidly into southern Germany. From then until mid-May, I made two or three flights a day, seven days a week, hauling fuel to supply the tanks of Patton's fast-moving army. The fuel was transported in five-gallon "jerry cans," each full can weighing forty-three pounds. The crew had to load and unload several hundred cans each trip. The four of us would typically carry two jerry cans at once. I grew to be in very excellent shape.

One day, I was the lead plane of an element of three planes carrying fuel into Bavaria. We were above the clouds for most of the flight. Descending through the overcast sky, we seemed to have entered another reality. Directly in front of us was the incredible castle at Neuschwanstein, a true fairy-tale castle.

The place seemed enchanted. Heightening our amazement, there appeared—just at that moment, out of nowhere—a plane with no propellers, moving twice as fast as any plane we had ever seen.

We realized it was flying straight at us. It scared the hell out of us. We had never seen a plane fly so fast. The only planes we knew without propellers were gliders. But this wasn't a glider. It was a German jet fighter. It sped past us, probably on a test flight. After the Germans surrendered, I saw a lot more of those jets. Our airfield in Melun was where the jets were taken apart and put back together again like a big jigsaw puzzle as the Allied engineers tried to understand how they worked.

On a beautiful afternoon in early May, my crew and I were lying in a grassy field in southern Bavaria waiting for a truck to come so we could unload our cargo. Our radio operator always kept the frequency open so that we could receive messages. I'll never forget the moment he excitedly declared that the Germans had surrendered. We—like hundreds of thousands of people who fought for and supported the Allied cause—were joyous.

Though it was after dark when we left that Bavarian field to head back to home base, we flew with the image that there was now light at the end of what had been a very long and dark tunnel.

On the way home we saw the dazzling lights of Paris. I decided it was appropriate to take a victory tour. Using the Seine as a guide, I flew to the Place de la Concorde, dropped down to two hundred feet, and flew just above the treetops along the Champs-Élysees to the Arc de Triomphe—over the heads of hundreds of thousands of happy Parisians just beneath me. I flicked my landing lights on and off to celebrate the moment. It never occurred to me until later that there might have been some other wildly excited, crazy pilot who'd chosen that moment to fly down the Champs-Élysees—in the opposite direction.

Richard J. Redfern, a glider pilot whom I didn't know, was on the Champs-Élysees that night. He wrote a description of that evening for a glider pilot newsletter. My friend Patricia Overman later found it and read it to me.

> That was a wild night. Those lucky enough to be strolling along the Champs Elysees on VE Day evening can never forget the joyous, jam-packed crowds of people and how every person in uniform was a hero, and everyone wanted to shake your hand, buy you a drink, or give you a kiss. I was standing up near the Arc de Triomphe when I heard the crowd noise rise even higher. As I looked toward the Place de la Concorde, I saw with amazement what appeared to be a huge truck with very bright lights driving right through the crowd. Then I detected the familiar sound of a pair of engines and I could see that it was a C-47 with its landing lights on. That plane was flying down between the buildings with its props less than 30 feet (sic) above the crowd. Approaching the Arc de Triomphe, with props in low pitch and motors roaring, it pulled up, shining the lights on the Arc, and then disappeared into the darkness. The war in Europe was over— and the city of Paris had received one final salute from a troop carrier.

"That was me! He saw me!" I declared as Patricia read me the account. "That was me!"

Since the war with Germany was over, we were eager to learn when we could go home. No news was forthcoming. We continued routine flights, flying equipment from one place to another and transferring troops from one place to another. Once we were assigned to pick up concentration camp survivors and take them to Dresden, in the Russian sector of what became East Germany. They were Russian soldiers who had been captured by the Germans. As they came to the plane, they looked like apparitions, walking human scarecrows. They had sunken eyes and hollow cheeks. I didn't know men could be so thin and still be alive. I stood outside the door of the plane to help them in as they hobbled up to the steps. The first man to board the plane fell to his knees and kissed my boots.

I'd never felt such a welter of emotion—shame and pity mixed with riotous other emotions. I later learned that the Russian army had no tolerance for their own captured soldiers. They were executed because they had not fought to the death, a shocking, unfathomable display of inhumanity.

After Germany's surrender, and before my return home, I enjoyed several experiences. We were sent to a French air base in the Bordeaux region to help train French paratroopers. After flying all morning, providing prospective paratroopers their qualifying jumps, we were driven to a community center near the town square of the small village of Avord. We were treated to a lovely lunch of good food and fine wine from the area, one known as the Saint-Emilion or Saint-Estèphe region. This was my first experience with very good wines. And it was a wonderful experience indeed. After lunch every day, I would walk to the grassy town square and lie back against a tree until the truck came to take us back to base. On full stomachs, we'd spend the rest of the afternoon flying over the scenic Bordeaux countryside, dropping more French paratroopers. It was a very plum assignment.

In the middle of June 1945, orders arrived transferring me back to the United States. I was also granted a thirty-day home leave before having to return to active duty. It was widely presumed within our group that return to duty meant we would be sent to the Pacific for the final invasion of Japan. I was grateful for the leave, but did not look forward to a return to battle. We were, however, still at war.

Just before leaving France, I was assigned as the squadron's officer of the day. My responsibility was to ensure the safety and security of the base. That evening there were guards assigned to watch over our fenced-in, yet open-air warehouse of supplies and parts. It was raining when I got in a Jeep around midnight to drive out to check on them. I drove up to the first guard, who was huddled under some equipment trying to stay dry. He asked for the password. I gave the password.

Again, he asked for the password. This time as he raised his carbine, pointing it right at me.

I smelled liquor. He was as drunk as one could be and still be standing. I thought, "This is a hell of a note—to come through the war unscathed, only to be shot by a member of my own squadron just before leaving for home."

I asked him to point his gun somewhere else and gave him the password again. He wasn't able to comprehend anything.

Finally I said, "We're both getting wet. Why don't you hop in the Jeep and I'll take you back to the office where you can dry off."

"I can't abandon my post," he slurred.

"You're not abandoning your post," I said. "I'm the officer in charge, and I'm taking you off your post, so you don't have to worry."

He crawled into the Jeep and I took him to the office. Once I got him inside, I called the sergeant over.

"Take that gun away from this son of a bitch before he kills someone! Then have somebody take him to his barracks and put him in bed." The sergeant nodded. "And when he wakes up in the morning," I added, "tell him to keep his mouth shut."

I knew that if he said anything about the incident, I would have to properly file charges against him. Which meant that I would then have to stay in Europe for the court-martial. I felt sorry for the kid—a long way from home without a clue what he was doing here.

The sergeant did as I asked. We all wanted to go home.

I looked forward to the return flight to the States. Bernie, my regular copilot, had been given his own plane. However, with great displeasure, I learned that Major Rowerdink was slated to be my copilot. That meant long hours in the air sitting next to him, retracing the circuitous route that had brought me to Europe in December 1943.

We left France in early July. The flight down the west coast of Africa was uneventful until our approach to Roberts Field in Liberia. Rowerdink, who had so far been useless on the flight, was sitting in the copilot seat perusing the map of the area. It showed a mountain not too far from the airfield. He concluded that our navigator had made a mistake and was going to get us killed by flying into that mountain. Since he was a major and out-ranked me, he attempted to insist that we change course.

He and the navigator were in the midst of a very heated argument when I said, "Major, I am the pilot of this plane, and there-fore I am in charge. This navigator and I have flown together for a year and a half. He has gotten me safely through this war. I have total confidence in him. We are going to follow his route."

I had a very heavy pipe wrench under my seat that I was prepared, and maybe even eager, to use on him if he gave me any problems.

When we broke through the clouds, we had a nice view of the mountain several miles away—exactly where the navigator said it would be. Nothing further was said on the subject.

The rest of the journey went without incident until we reached Borinquen Field in Puerto Rico. I went into the operations building to check in after landing. The pilot who walked in behind me threw his keys on the desk and said, "I'm through! Get somebody else to fly that plane!" He explained that his plane had rolled over on its back in a thunderstorm coming in—and that that was the end of his flying.

I'd just flown through that same region of thunderstorms and happily missed such an experience.

We landed in the United States at Hunter Air Base in Savannah, Georgia. I was happy to be home. I walked to the operations building and turned in the keys of my fine plane. A group of us were put on a bus to Charleston, South Carolina, where we took an overnight train to Newark, New Jersey. We were transported by truck to Fort Dix. I received a thirty-day pass and was instructed to return in a month to be sent to the Pacific to take part in the invasion of Japan.

For the moment, however, I was heading to New York to see Flavil.

VIII

Home Again

Dressed in my uniform, I stepped out of a taxi in front of the elegant Park Avenue building. The doorman, initially suspicious, smiled when I mentioned that I was Flavil's husband. He said, "Mrs. Boyd is waiting for you upstairs." We hadn't seen each other for almost nineteen months. When the door opened, there was Flavil wearing a black dress. She was stunning. I remember thinking, "How beautiful" as I looked into her eyes. I was overwhelmed with love.

That evening, she took me to a little Italian restaurant in Greenwich Village, where she often went to meet her artist friends. It had an open kitchen where we could watch the food being prepared. Entranced by Flavil's laughing eyes, I didn't pay attention to the chefs—in fact, I don't even remember what I ate. I do remember that Evelyn kindly let us have the apartment to ourselves for the night. It was a happy reunion indeed.

I was in New York only two days. On one of them—July 28—a B-25 bomber flew into the Empire State Building. Three crewmen on board were killed, along with eleven people in the building. I read that the pilot became disoriented on approach to

Newark Airport because there was zero visibility in thick fog. He turned right at the Chrysler Building instead of left, and flew into the north side of the iconic building, between Floors 78 and 80. After my vertigo over the English Channel, I understood how that could happen. I felt sorry for the deaths. The tragedy was also a sharp reminder that I was heading back to war in a little less than thirty days.

Flavil and I left New York by train. We went to Macclenny to see Mother and Jean, who were living together in Mother's house. Jean's husband, Morris Dowling, was still overseas in the service. Most of the boys I'd grown up with had gone to war. I was sad to learn that Robert Wolf, my friend and next-door neighbor, had been killed, shot down flying for the US Navy in the Pacific. Amazingly, I think Robert was the only fatality from our town.

After a few days in Macclenny, Flavil and I went on to Jacksonville Beach, where we had two wonderful weeks of rest and relaxation. We were there on August 6 when we learned that an atomic bomb had been dropped on Hiroshima. I was both horrified and elated. I thought it would force Japan to surrender, sparing me a return to war. But I was saddened by the massive death toll and destruction. With a bomb that powerful, I wondered what the future held.

On August 14, Japan agreed to an unconditional surrender. The war was officially over. I had not only survived, but survived intact.

The peace caused me to reflect on my war experience. I recalled watching a play in a London theater, the sound of bombs exploding nearby. The actors continued without pause, the audience sitting calmly. It was an example—one of many I witnessed—of the impressive fortitude of the British. They would spend night after night below ground in Tube stations to be safe from the constant German bombing, then come out each morning to go off to work amidst the devastation.

Ever foremost in my mind was my gratitude and esteem for the RAF. Its pilots had been unfailingly gracious and fearless. In addition to welcoming me as one of their own, they had saved my life.

I was proud to have served, and to have done my part. I was also grateful that I hadn't had to kill anyone. I know I would have if called upon to do so, but I was glad I did not have to carry such knowledge for the rest of my life.

I was sad about friends I had lost. Yet I was able to affirm that "that was then, this is now." I was ready to move on. I knew there were plenty of men and women who weren't as lucky.

At the end of my thirty-day leave, I was a passenger on my first-ever commercial flight. I flew on National Airlines from Jacksonville to Newark, to muster out of the military at Fort Dix. During processing, the army offered to pay me ninety-six dollars a month if I agreed to stay in the Reserves. If I accepted, I was required to fly four hours a month to maintain my status as an active pilot who could be recalled immediately in case of another war. With law school on the horizon, ninety-six dollars a month sounded very useful. I agreed. On my return to Macclenny, Flavil and I packed our belongings and moved to Charlottesville.

Like the Army Air Corps, the University of Virginia law school required two years of college for entrance. I doubted, however, that the university would be as willing to overlook my two failed classes. I was pleasantly surprised when the dean of the law school, Dean Ribble, looked at my transcript and allowed me to explain that my attitude and situation at this point were much improved. I said that I desperately wanted a legal education. He acknowledged that my grades were not good enough for him to accept me into law school at that time, but he offered a generous compromise.

"If you take one semester at the university in the college of arts and sciences and do well," he said, "I'll have a place for you in the law school next February."

I assured him that that certainly would be the case.

The culture of the University of Virginia was quite different from that of the University of Florida. Florida students wore anything that appealed to them. At Virginia, a coat and tie were required when on "the grounds," as the campus was called. The school, which was all male, expected students to be gentlemen in all circumstances. This included adhering to a code of honor that said, "No student shall lie, cheat, or steal." Violations were reported and enforced by students, each case being decided by the student council. There was only one possible consequence to a finding of guilt: immediate expulsion. The council's decision was final. I know of only one student who cheated and was expelled while I was there.

With the code of honor both respected and enforced by the students, we were often left on our own without a proctor during tests. We were trusted—and we trusted each other—to be honest and honorable. We could go outside for a cigarette and even talk to each other if we wanted. I greatly enjoyed the culture of honor, and embraced it as a code to guide my life from that point forward.

At the end of the semester I brought my grades to Dean Ribble. I'd taken economics, public speaking, and history, and done very well in all three. He greeted me warmly and told me to plan on entering law school the following Tuesday.

Law school, which normally took three years, was condensed to two years for a time immediately after the war. I started in February 1946, in a class of about two hundred students, most cut from the same cloth as me—young, white men, fresh from military service. The exceptions were two women and two foreigners, one from London and one from Hong Kong. As a group we were convivial, enjoying each other's company. Our courses were interesting, and we were serious in our studies.

Yet not every student made the grade. In fact, one, Hardy Mathieson, who later became the dearest friend of my life, failed a six-hour course in torts. He was a man of stubborn determination. He went to the professor after receiving the failing grade and argued his case in a somewhat belligerent tone. After an extended discussion, the professor said with finality, "Mr. Mathieson, this university is not big enough for the both of us, and I have tenure. Goodbye!"

The study of law was rich with history and precedence. I found it fascinating. I was able to explore my wartime interest in aviation by working with a professor on a self-guided course in aviation law. I learned a lot, especially about subsidies, the largest body of aviation law in the United States. I did well in that course, as I did in my other courses. Although never a great scholar, I was on the dean's list every semester.

Flavil and I lived just down the hill from the law school in a small, one-bedroom apartment. Our building had nine apartments in all, eight of them filled with married law students, the ninth occupied by the building's owner, Miss Anna Barringer.

Miss Anna was a member of the First Families of Virginia, a fact she never let one forget. Her father had been dean of the medical school at UVA. Miss Anna was in her fifties and had a very imperious look.

She kept a purse and hat near the front door. When her doorbell rang, she put on her hat and carried her purse to open the door. If she didn't like the person she saw, she would announce, "I'm very sorry. I'm just on my way out. You may come some other time." Then she would close the door with a bang.

Miss Anna took a liking to me. She reduced our rent from $45.00 to $35.00 a month in exchange for my cleaning the hall floors once a week. That $10.00 reduction was helpful. In addition to the $96.00 I got from the Army Reserves, I earned $25.00 a month from the law library, where I stacked books and ran off announcements on the duplicating machine. Fortunately, all of my educational expenses, tuition and books, were paid for by a wonderful new government program known as the G.I. Bill. It made a college education possible for thousands of returning servicemen.

A bonus of my Army Reserve requirement to fly four hours a month was the regular opportunity to fly from Charlottesville to an air base with a commissary. There, I would buy food at considerably less cost than at our local grocery store.

Flavil, creative and industrious as ever, brought in a fair amount of money coloring Currier & Ives prints. She used a production line approach, spreading the prints out on the dining room table and painting in the skies, then rooftops, then tree trunks, and so on. Currier & Ives prints sold well in both stores and catalogs, and she earned a good bit of money.

A number of the other wives in our building were also painting for Currier & Ives. Like Flavil, many were pregnant. Flavil painted joyously until our son, Mark, was born on April 18, 1946, at the University Hospital. Flavil proved to be a devoted, protective mother, generous with her time and talents.

Our one big purchase was a car. Neither Flavil nor I had ever owned a car, but my dear uncle Lucius, in Massachusetts, was getting too old to drive. Aunt Agnes offered us their car at a very reasonable price.

With our new mobility, Flavil got involved in selling Fine Art Sterling. It was a direct-sales business. A woman would invite her friends to a house party for the purpose of buying new flatware from Flavil. I would watch Mark in the evening while Flavil went to her parties. She was a good saleswoman, and the timing was fortuitous. Many of the husbands of the women she met with were about to graduate from law school. Their wives were interested in having nice things like flatware to set up their new homes. We acquired ten nice place settings ourselves in the process.

Although I didn't graduate from law school until February 1948, I took and passed the Virginia bar exam in the summer of 1947 and started my job search. One of my first interviews in Washington, DC, was with the Civil Aeronautics Board (CAB), the government agency that regulated the airlines and investigated plane accidents, among other things. With my aviation experience and my studies in aviation law, I thought this would be a good fit. The board, however, didn't agree. (Ironically, I was to become a CAB board member twelve years later.)

Because I was interested in government, I arranged visits to Washington, DC, law firms by contacting UVA law school alumni working there. In one of the larger firms, which covered several floors of an older office building, a senior partner took me on a tour. Downstairs in the library, surrounded by bookcases and ensconced in a small carrel, I met their newest hire, a Harvard grad and former editor of the *Harvard Law Review*. I thought, "If one of the top Ivy League law scholars gets stuck in the library, where would they stick me?" My interest in Washington law firms quickly dissipated.

Flavil pushed for me to look for a job in New York City. She had loved living there while I was away at war. I said no. I thought New York City was no place to raise a family. We planned on having six kids. (Mark turned out to be our one and only.)

Shortly before graduation, Dean Ribble called me into his office to say that a UVA graduate from the class of '37 had called from Miami, looking to hire a new associate for his law firm. The dean knew I was from Florida and offered to recommend me if I was interested. Soon I was on my way to Miami to interview at the law firm of Smathers, Thompson, Maxwell, and Dyer. I met with one of the partners, Mr. Meister. We talked for about forty-five minutes about the law, my family, and local matters. Things went well.

"You can work here if you'd like," he said. "The starting salary is $125 a month, but since you're married, we'll pay you $150."

That was lower than I had in mind. But there was potential, he said, for substantial raises. I accepted the job.

IX

Miami

The day after graduation, Flavil and I packed the car, bundled up two-year-old Mark, and moved to Miami. I knew Miami and environs would be very different from Macclenny. Northern Florida, where I was raised, is Southern to the core. It's also a land of pine forests, hardwood trees, and citrus groves. South Florida has the Everglades, swamps, cypress trees, beaches, and palm trees. Culturally, South Florida is more like the North, populated mostly by Yankees looking for sunshine and warmth.

Smathers Thompson, the second-largest law firm in Miami, had twelve attorneys. I was assigned to share a small office with two other new hires. I was pleasantly surprised to find that one of them was Hardy Mathieson, the law student who'd been forced out of UVA by his torts professor. My other deskmate was Richard Russell Paige, a Harvard Law graduate. Dick was a warm, affable person with an excellent legal mind. Our three desks were all pushed together in the small space, and we shared a secretary. The three of us became good friends. I was especially close to Hardy, a truly wonderful person who became like a brother to me.

The firm had a diverse law practice, but focused mostly on commercial or business law. The work assigned to me was interesting—though not exactly gripping. In my first few months, I worked for Mr. Meister, who, among other things, was the city attorney for Miami Shores.

I drafted city council resolutions on such important issues as trash pickup and delivery, and pet leash laws. Even less rousing was doing real estate title searches, which was extremely detail oriented. One thing I am not is a detail man. I had to identify every corner, mete, and bound, carefully making sure that every comma and semicolon was correctly placed. It was the most boring work I've ever done.

I did, however, learn the history of land ownership while doing property title searches. Florida was a Spanish territory from 1513 to 1821. For a title to be valid, it had to be traced continuously from the Crown of Spain to the owners in the current transaction. Of particular interest to me, given my love of history, I learned that Julia Tuttle and a boxful of orange blossoms played an essential role in the development of Miami.

In 1891, Mrs. Tuttle, a widow from Cleveland, bought one square mile north of the mouth of the Miami River—640 fertile acres. What is now downtown Miami was then named Fort Dallas. Henry Flagler was building the new Florida East Coast Railway from Jacksonville down to West Palm Beach. Mrs. Tuttle tried to persuade him to continue the railway another seventy miles southward to Miami. In this, she failed.

A few years later, Florida was hit by several consecutive freezes that destroyed nearly all the citrus in the state—except in the Miami area. Mrs. Tuttle sent Flagler a box of fresh, unharmed orange blossoms, with an invitation to visit the "freeze-proof" area. Her ploy, plus the offer to give him half of her land, enabled her to finally succeed in achieving her original goal. The extended railway was completed in April 1896. The newly renamed town, Miami, was incorporated three months later.

Flavil, Mark, and I rented a furnished house in a development recently built on the edge of the Everglades. Five miles to the east was downtown Miami and my office. Two blocks to the west was the swamp. I took the bus into work each day and left Flavil the car so that she would not feel isolated so far from town.

Our monthly rent of $95.00 was covered by my $96.00 monthly Army Reserve check. That left my salary of $150.00 a month to live on. It was enough to get by on, but we couldn't afford a telephone or the newspaper. We thought it a luxury to eat meat once a week.

Six months after we moved to Miami, we bought an acre-and-a-quarter lot for three thousand dollars, exactly the amount Flavil had saved from her teaching salary and what I'd sent home during the war. The lot, south of the town of South Miami, was empty except for a small concrete pump house and a line of Australian pines that served as a windbreak. It was in the middle of nowhere.

Now the challenge was how to build a house having spent all our money buying the lot. Flavil, with more optimism than wisdom, concluded that she and I could build a house together. Notwithstanding my concerns about my own capacities, I acceded to her plan. I didn't have a better one.

We checked the building codes and learned that we had to have at least a thousand square feet under a roof—as well as various requirements to tie the roof down to protect the building in case of hurricanes. Flavil drew up plans for a 40-by-25-foot rectangle with two bedrooms, one bath, a living room, a dining room, a kitchen, and a small entrance hall. We started figuring what it would cost to build it. Visiting building supply stores in the area, looking for the cheapest concrete, lumber, wiring, windows, and so on, we estimated we could build the house for about $4,500. Mother graciously offered to take out a $5,000 mortgage on her home in Macclenny if we could make the $100-a-month mortgage payments. We agreed. With the aid of Mother's money, we broke ground.

Flavil enlisted the help of Nick Fiorentino, a retired ships' carpenter from Brooklyn who lived with his daughter across the street from our rented house. Nick would knock on neighbors' doors offering to fix things, just to stay active and to have company. He was full of help and advice about our project. Initially, he insisted that we dig a basement, refusing to grasp that South Florida was really an ancient coral reef that was now just a few feet above sea level. Beneath three inches of dirt was solid limestone. Four feet farther down was water. Once he finally accepted that there were no basements in South Florida, he became a very helpful asset.

Flavil spent all day, every day, working on the house. Mark, who was only two, was as helpful as he could be as her apprenticed helper. I did what I could before and after work. We hired a mason to lay the concrete block walls while I served as the gofer, mixing cement and hauling cinder blocks. Once the walls were up, Flavil began stuccoing the exterior. Every morning before work, I would mix a wheelbarrow of stucco to get her started.

After the walls were completed, two young friends and I put up the roof rafters and laid the 1-foot-by-4-inch tongue-and-groove sheeting across them. The sheeting had to be nailed to the rafters, a task accomplished by Flavil with enthusiastic help from Mark. Adept at hammering nails, he was unconcerned with whether they actually encountered the rafters. As long as we lived there, we could see nails protruding from the ceiling, marking his creative handiwork.

Flavil and I were a good team. She painted the outside, and I framed the inside. Flavil hung the lower Sheetrock and laid the floor tile, and I hung the upper Sheetrock. Nick took care of the windows and the doors, which was good, because having every-thing level and square was not my talent.

Once the windows were in and the doors were almost ready to be hung, we moved in. At night I used a chair to prop the front door in place to keep the wild animals out. I hadn't yet figured out how to install the shower, so we showered in the paved car-port after dark, using a garden hose hanging from the rafters. As we continued to work on finishing the interior, we found that hanging wallpaper could test even the strongest of marriages. We ended up making a pact that our marriage was indeed more important than the wallpaper.

We built a patio behind the house that was completely screened in, designed to keep out the squadrons of mosquitoes that patrolled the area. They showed up around dusk every sum-mer evening. They often came in dark swarms like a D-Day inva-sion.

For several months we did nothing but work. We would go to bed utterly exhausted. It was quiet out there at night. There were few other houses around. Few cars drove past on the road that ran in front of the house. We would listen to the call of the whip-poor-wills in the pine grove behind our property. We were so dog-tired that we would just lie there and laugh until we fell asleep. It took eight months to finish. It required us to squeeze every nickel and work long, endless days. But I think we never had a happier time in our lives.

I enjoyed my four hours of Reserve flying every month. I would take off on a weekend afternoon and fly east over the Atlantic or southwest to the Keys. Flying west toward the sun as it sank into the Gulf of Mexico, I enjoyed watching the light of the sunset reflect off the clouds, coloring the water around the islands below shades of pink, red, and orange.

One of my most memorable Reserve flights involved a trip to San Francisco. I stopped in Arizona for fuel. On takeoff I had trouble getting the lift needed to become airborne because the extremely high heat made the air so thin. A few feet short of the end of the runway, the plane lifted. It was sufficient to get airborne, but my wheels didn't clear the four-foot fence at the end of the airport. I didn't crash, but part of the fence dangled from my landing gear for a while. Late in the afternoon, I flew down into the Grand Canyon. There were no rules restricting it then. It was a truly thrilling experience.

Once the house was finished, Flavil and I concentrated on landscaping. I thought a semicircular drive lined with coconut palms would be attractive. Hardy offered to give us as many coconut trees as I wanted. His family owned most of Key Biscayne, on which they had the largest coconut plantation in the continental United States.

Since there were only three inches of dirt above the limestone, planting a dozen coconut trees would require significant effort. I decided dynamite was called for. I'd never dealt with dynamite, but having the education of a lawyer, I thought I knew enough to be able to place dynamite in a hole. I dug as far as I could with a pickax, and then used a hand drill and a hammer to go a little deeper. I carefully placed a quarter of a stick in the two-foot-deep hole. I covered the hole with a wooden pallet, on top of which I put a wheelbarrow filled with concrete blocks to contain the blast. I asked Flavil to take Mark inside. I lit the fuse and prudently moved a safe distance away.

Florida has an illustrious history of rocket launches. Mine, I think, was the first suborbital wheelbarrow flight. The wooden pallet, wheelbarrow, and concrete blocks shot into the air. One concrete block landed on our roof, another on the pump house. The wheelbarrow didn't survive. To say Flavil failed to appreciate my foray into space exploration would be an enormous understatement. I hired an expert to finish the job.

While I was planting palm trees and building the house, I was also learning the practice of law, finding my way around the courthouse, and getting to know Miami, a dynamic place in 1949. The population was exploding with transplants from the North and with returning World War II vets who had been stationed there during the war.

With about 250,000 people, it was still small enough that I got to know the mayor, the city council members, and the judges. I also knew the traffic cop outside our law office. He was a congenial guy who smiled and laughed with everyone. He was so popular that he ran for Congress and won.

In 1950, one of the partners of the firm, George Smathers, ran for the US Senate. George was the whole package. He was handsome, intelligent, articulate, and a former WWII Marine Corps officer. He'd also served as a prosecuting attorney and as a two-term congressman.

I'm not sure why he picked me, but George asked me to take a six-month leave of absence from the law firm to work on his campaign. I can only assume that he saw my aptitude for or the interest I had in politics. Maybe it was because I knew something about northern Florida. I readily accepted. I figured I needed my own clients if I was ever going to make much money or be able to practice a more interesting brand of law. A political campaign would mix me with a lot of people around the state. There was no question that I would enjoy the game.

George ran as a Democrat against the incumbent Claude Pepper, also a Democrat. Pepper's left-leaning political views had fallen out of favor, as had his earlier support of the Soviet Union. This was at the start of the Cold War. The country was in no mood for a senator who, after a visit to Moscow, said that Stalin was "a man Americans could trust." Although Senator Pepper was vulnerable, he would not be easily defeated. He had been in the Senate since 1936. He was influential in passing important Depression- and war-era legislation, and had been a good friend of both Franklin and Eleanor Roosevelt. An intelligent, articulate, Harvard-educated lawyer, he was an excellent and engaging storyteller. The common view among political pundits was that Smathers didn't stand a chance.

Pepper was expected to win Dade County, Florida's most densely populated area, by a wide margin, thanks to its large Jewish community and its active labor unions. Both groups loved Senator Pepper, who was staunchly pro-Israel and pro-labor, and these constituents were people who got out and voted.

I was assigned to a part of northern Dade County that included Miami Springs, Hialeah, and Opa Locka (the abbreviation of the Seminole Indian place-name, Opa-tisha-wocka-locka). Sloan McCrea, the Dade County campaign manager, other young professionals, a few college students, and I worked out of an office in the back room of Faber's drugstore on Coral Way near Coral Gables. Some worked full time, others part time. We met at 8:00 a.m., six mornings a week to strategize and focus our efforts.

I traveled extensively throughout my area to meet with supporters, to look for endorsements, and to find people who could be helpful to the campaign. We needed volunteers who would pass out literature, bumper stickers, and yard signs. We also needed people to phone voters and to campaign for George at shopping centers on weekends. We sought volunteers who would organize rides for those who couldn't get to the polls on their own on voting day. It was common for me not to return home until after midnight—only to get up at 7:00 the next day to start out again. Those were grueling but energizing days. The long hours were eased somewhat by driving the brand new Packard that the campaign provided me.

With Dade County solidly in Pepper's corner, our goal was not to win there, but to neutralize the vote in its precincts. We scheduled a speech for George in Miami and brainstormed ways to attract a big crowd. I suggested a free public barbecue. The good news: everyone loved the idea. The bad news: Sloan put me in charge of it.

The start of the big day was auspicious. The weather was sunny and pleasant. The vacant land I'd acquisitioned near the airport for the event was ready with a stage, tables, parking, and food for three thousand people. Folks began to arrive . . . and arrive, and arrive. We had at least twice the number we expected. I grabbed every available campaign worker and sent them off to every barbecue stand in Dade County with orders to buy everything available and return ASAP. We called Coca-Cola. They sent out several more trucks loaded with cold drinks. George gave a resounding speech. The day was a huge success. The press was duly impressed. And everyone got something to eat.

As the event began to wind down and people began to leave, I began to breathe easier. Until I saw the god-awful mess left in the event's wake. Acres of bottles, paper plates, napkins, and heaven knows what else was strewn wildly about. I stood in the sea of litter trying to figure out what to do. It seemed a hopeless situation.

One of our college-aged campaign workers approached. "I'll tell you what, Alan," he said. "My fraternity will clean this place up—if you buy us a few kegs of beer."

Such a bargain. It was win-win all around.

The barbecue was a success—as was the campaign. In Dade County, Pepper's potential landslide was limited to a narrow 947-vote victory. Smathers ended up beating Pepper in the Democratic primary. He went on to easily win in the general election, taking 76 percent of the statewide vote.

Several years after his Senate defeat, Claude was elected to Congress, representing the Miami Beach area in the House of Representatives. He held that office from 1963 until he died in 1989. I met him after I moved to Washington. We became very good friends even though he was aware of my role in his Senate defeat. He had a great sense of humor and loved a good joke. I liked him very much. Claude Pepper was a great servant of the people and a wonderful man.

X

Korea

On June 25, 1950, while I was working on George's campaign, North Korea, strongly supported by Russia and China, invaded South Korea. The United Nations Security Council passed a resolution against the aggression and authorized United Nations military intervention to stop it. The United States provided almost 90 percent of the United Nation troops. President Harry Truman ordered more than 970 Reserve units back to active duty, including mine, the 435th Troop Carrier Group of the US Air Force.

I hadn't planned on another war. I had friends, including a county commissioner, who used strategies to avoid active duty. I could have asked Senator Smathers to get me out of it. But I had signed an agreement with the military after World War II ended, and felt obligated to uphold my end of the deal. On March 1, 1951, I was reinstated as a captain in the US Air Force. Because of the credit I had for two thousand flying hours and nineteen months of overseas duty, I was not sent to Korea. I was assigned instead to be a flight instructor at Miami Airport. The west side of the airport was converted into a military base, and the east remained civilian. I could go to war each morning and come home to Flavil and Mark each night.

Surprisingly, my job as flight instructor was more dangerous and more stressful than much of my overseas duty in WWII. I instructed active and inactive Reserve pilots. My job was to qualify them on the twin-engine C-46 Commando. The Curtiss C-46 was bigger than the C-47; it had several unflattering nicknames, including The Whale, The Curtiss Calamity, The Plumber's Nightmare (perhaps because of numerous problems with fuel leaks that would cause it to spontaneously explode while flying), and . . . The Flying Coffin. It was large and cumbersome. An extremely large rudder and tail surface area made it a difficult plane to handle in a crosswind. Both pilot and copilot needed to have a firm grip on the controls.

My goal as instructor was to help the men qualify to fly C-46s, not to wash them out of the program. Many had not flown since they'd graduated from single-engine flight school, and had never learned to fly a twin-engine plane. The pilots with twin-engine experience hadn't flown since WWII. And many of them were scared of the C-46. This was not conducive to a relaxed atmosphere in the cockpit. I tried hard to maintain a calm disposition to help combat the trainees' anxiety and fear.

Most rudiments of twin-engine flight were easy to teach. They were not that stressful. Learning how to land, fly on one engine while airborne, and recover from stalls—I could teach those skills well. There was, however, one dangerous situation a trainee was required to handle as part of their qualifying flight. On takeoff, sitting with them in the cockpit, I would cut off one engine. This caused some terrible gyrations. I was literally putting my life in the hands of pilots who were afraid of the plane. Some pilots lost it, challenging me to grab the controls before we encountered a fatal disaster. I was constantly on pins and needles, scared as hell. On occasion, we ran off the runway. By August, I'd developed a stomach ulcer so severe, I was taken off flying status for a period of time.

Thankfully, I was reassigned to the 435th group headquarters as assistant operations officer. The 435th group was part of the Western Hemisphere Defense Force. Our group's mission was to be prepared to transport the 17th Airborne Division, based in Fort Campbell, Kentucky, anywhere from the Panama Canal to northern Alaska, in the case of an invasion. Because of this, I had the opportunity to fly to many places I'd never been.

In spring 1952, I flew to the Thule Air Base in Greenland. From there we were to fly equipment for a secret "weather base" to be set up on sea ice, three hundred miles from the North Pole, to "monitor the weather in Russia." Thule was then a secret base used for refueling the B-52 bombers carrying nuclear bombs. The United States kept B-52s constantly in the air over the Arctic Circle, ready to launch a retaliatory attack on the Soviet Union in case of nuclear war.

The term *Cold War* was appropriate for Thule. The lowest recorded temperature in Greenland was minus 87 degrees Fahrenheit. When there, I threw a glass of water into the air. It turned to ice, like a frozen waterfall, before hitting the ground. It was so cold that the screw caps in the fifty-five-gallon barrels of jet fuel used for refueling the B-52s would freeze tight. A worker on the base, "Blowtorch Morgan," had the job of heating the drums of fuel with a blowtorch so the caps could be unscrewed. His was a lonely job, indeed.

The evening we arrived in Thule, the temperature was about 50 degrees below zero. I took my flight bag to my quarters, which looked and felt like the inside of an icebox, and headed to the mess hall. It was open twenty-four hours a day because the B-52 crews worked around the clock. I got a pleasant surprise when the man in front of me in line turned around.

It was Wally Boggs, my best man in Altus when Flavil and I married. We hadn't seen each other since graduating from flight school. He was now Lieutenant Colonel Boggs, commanding B-52s. We had a great time catching up.

The weather station was to be set up on the ice off the coast of Greenland. A small plane was sent to verify that the ice there was thick enough to support our heavy C-119 transports. The report came back that the ice was eight feet thick and strong enough to land a locomotive. We landed on the ice with no problem—except that the planes' brakes were ineffective on ice.

The temperature gauge read 54 degrees below zero as we unloaded. The equipment for the weather station included a dog-sled and sled dogs, as well as a "duck"—an open vehicle with tank-like tracks instead of wheels. Blowtorch Morgan backed the duck off the plane and parked it. Then for some reason, he took off his gloves. As he got out of the driver's seat, he grabbed the windshield to steady himself. The warmth of his bare hand shattered the incredibly frigid glass, slicing his hand to the bone. It was so cold, his blood froze. We could look into the cut and see his muscles, tendons, and bone as if he were a cadaver. We got him into the cockpit, wrapped his hand, and quickly flew him back to the infirmary in Thule.

On the flight back to Miami, we lost all electrical power and the use of all our instruments. Our radio operator became hysterical. We didn't know it at the time, but he had just been transferred back from war duty in Korea, the sole survivor of a C-119 crash. We finally got him calmed down. Fortunately, it was a clear day with good visibility and we got home safely.

As assistant group operations officer, I was given primary responsibility for developing a plan and organizing the logistics to airlift the 17th Airborne Division for a massive maneuver in the fall of 1952. The 435th and other troop carrier units were to fly the paratroopers from their base in Kentucky and drop them around Elmendorf, Alaska, in a scenario pretending that an invasion had taken place there.

Planes would have to fly to Fort Campbell, Kentucky, from Miami and other bases around the country, pick up paratroopers there, and then fly up to Alaska, making several refueling stops on the way. I made several trips in advance to Alaska to check out aspects of the proposed exercise.

I inspected the airfields we would use as refueling stops to assess their capabilities. It was essential that the plane arrivals be evenly spaced so they wouldn't overwhelm the refueling bases, especially Watson Lake, in the Yukon, which could handle only one plane every thirty minutes. I had to route almost a hundred planes carrying thousands of men through that bottleneck in just over twenty-four hours.

The US military can take priority over civilian air routes by declaring a military necessity. Knowing there could be a significant problem, I went through the proper military channels to request that the maneuver be designated as such a necessity, thereby preventing dangerous congestion at Watson Lake. The Pentagon, however, responded in the negative.

When the time for the exercise arrived, I flew to Fort Campbell to make sure everything went well. Things started okay, but then we suffered delays because of air traffic from the Kansas City airport. I could see the domino effect was causing chaos and jeopardizing the safety and success of the entire exercise.

"To hell with this," I thought. I called air traffic control. "I'm declaring a military necessity for this maneuver."

I knew this would have repercussions in the Pentagon. "You're going to get a call," I told my sergeant. "Tell whoever it is that you have no idea where I am. That I've left and didn't tell you where I was going. But tell them you will be sure to give me the message as soon as you can find me."

Within two hours our phone started ringing. The sergeant answered. It was the Pentagon wanting to know where I was, and what was going on.

Following my order he replied, "Captain Boyd left about two hours ago, and didn't tell me where he was going." He was commanded to find me and tell me to withdraw the military necessity immediately.

"Forget it," I told him. "You'll be able to 'find me' when our last plane is off the ground."

I went back to the barracks and got some sleep. The rest of the planes took off on schedule. All went according to plan with one exception: one plane crashed into the water approaching Alaska, killing everyone on board. I never learned why.

To no one's surprise, within a few days I received a letter from air force headquarters outlining events and demanding that I reply by endorsement, meaning a formal response that would travel through the proper channels to headquarters. I wrote a courteous response in which I outlined the reasons for what I had done. I expressed my appreciation for the cooperation I had gotten from air force headquarters. I felt fairly tranquil about the situation, as my tour of duty was coming to an end in three weeks. I never heard another thing about the matter. But to my surprise, I was promoted to major. I was discharged in December 1952. I had been in the army for eleven years. I figured I had paid my dues to Uncle Sam and decided it was time to leave the Reserves.

PHOTOS

My mother, Jennie Elizabeth Stephenson.

My father and mother, Clarence Stafford Boyd and
Jennie Elizabeth Stephenson Boyd, circa 1921.

My father holding me, circa 1922.

My sister Jean and me, circa 1931.

My high school senior picture, 1939.

Flavil Townsend, close to the time I first saw her.

In uniform with my wings, 1943.

My plane, Wishwell E, loaded with paratroopers, waiting to take off on the evening of June 5, 1944.

Nurse and crew loading wounded into my plane.

The line of crosses represents the number of evacuation flights my plane made in the combat zone. My crew and I were very busy.

Flavil and me in
Charlottesville, 1946.

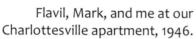
Flavil, Mark, and me at our
Charlottesville apartment, 1946.

Flavil and Mark leading the "baby boom" parade, on the
grounds of the University of Virginia, 1947.

The concrete block pump house on the site of our lot south of Miami, 1948.

Mark teaching me how to mix stucco.

Mark helping me put on the roof.

The first palm tree!

It was a wonderful time.

Thank goodness Flavil enjoyed my humor because I
sure couldn't dance.

Najeeb Halaby and I made sure the CAB and the FAA
went in the same direction.

President Johnson handing me a pen used in the signing of the
Highway Beautification Bill, October 22, 1965 with Lady Bird
Johnson looking on.

Being sworn in as Secretary of the Department of Transportation, January 16, 1967 with Flavil, the President and Mrs. Johnson.

Declaring the official launch of the department of transportation behind the new triskelion insignia on the podium, April 1, 1967.

Friends suggested that I generated the hot air
that filled the balloon I flew in during Transportation Day
on the Mall, April 1, 1967.

At a staff retreat for the new leaders of the new department.
From left to right, John Robson, John Sweeney, A. Sheffer Lang,
Langhorne Bond, me, Everett Hutchinson, William Mckee, Low-
ell Bridwell, Alan Dean, Cecil Mackey (behind), Willard Smith,
Paul Sitton, Joseph McCann, Donald Agger.

President Johnson standing in front of his Cabinet in 1967, from left to right around the table they are: Dean Rusk, Robert McNamara, Lawrence O'Brien, Orville Freeman, Willard Wirtz, Robert Weaver, me (standing), John Gardiner, Alexander Trowbridge, Stewart Udall, Ramsey Clark, Henry Fowler.

President Johnson was the most intense listener I ever met.

Flavil and me in Hawaii.

Entertaining in the dining room of the Illinois Central private car. Flavil in the foreground, then left to right, Muriel Newman, Elizabeth Paepcke, me, and Joy Rasin.

With President Carter during the Bermuda Air treaty
negotiations in 1977.

In Egypt with Flavil. We loved to travel together.

With Mark and his wife, Nancy, and my delightful grandchildren,
Alan and Heather, August, 2014.

On the runway at Membury on June, 6, 2014, the 70th
anniversary of D-day with my son, Mark, and his wife, Nancy.

Receiving a standing ovation from the other Secretaries of
Transportation in attendance at the celebration of the 50th
Anniversary year of the department. From left to right,
the current Secretary, Anthony R. Foxx, Mary E. Peters,
Norman Y. Mineta, Rodney E. Slater, Andrew H. Card, Jr.,
James H. Burnley IV, and me.

XI

Political Ambitions

After my discharge, I believed that my services with Smathers Thompson were worth more than they did. We parted ways.

Hardy and Dick had started their own law firm in my absence, and invited me to join. Mathieson, Paige and Boyd had an office three floors below Smathers Thompson. There were no hard feelings on either side. In fact, Smathers Thompson referred clients to us that they couldn't represent for one reason or another.

I had my own office and my own secretary, and we hired a law student who turned out not to be worth the powder it would have taken to blow him up. By the end of the first year, after paying all my expenses, including new law books for our library, I had earned a grand total of $420. Fortunately, Flavil had gone back to teaching now that Mark was old enough to start school. She supported the family while I tried to get my law practice going.

In September 1953, Florida's governor, Dan McCarty, died from a heart attack. The president of the state senate, Charley Johns, became acting governor. The Florida Constitution required a special election for the balance of the term. Charley announced that he wanted to keep the job.

I knew a lot about Charley Johns. He was from Starke, about thirty miles from Macclenny. He was not distinguished as a gifted man, nor was he the sort of man I could support as my governor. To give you a sense of him, later in 1956 as a state legislator, Charley chaired what would be known as the Johns Committee. He investigated Communists, homosexuals, and civil rights supporters within the Florida state university system. His committee forced more than three hundred teachers, administrators, and students out of Florida schools. People said of him later that he was so crooked, he had to be screwed into bed at night.

Not long after Charley announced that he would run for governor, I received a call from LeRoy "Roy" Collins, another Democratic state senator who had decided to run for governor.

"Harold Vann suggested I call you," Roy said to me by way of introduction. "I was wondering if you'd join Harold as co-chair for my campaign in Dade County."

Harold Vann was a friend whom I'd met while working on George Smathers's campaign. We were both WWII vets, lawyers, and Air Force Reservists. Like me, he'd just returned from active duty. I called Harold, who described Roy as intelligent, well spoken, and a good leader. After meeting Roy, I was impressed, and I agreed to join his campaign. Harold and I had contacts all around the county, and we assembled a lively, enthusiastic campaign staff.

In the course of the campaign, Roy and Charley agreed to a televised debate on WYVJ Channel 4 in Miami. In 1954, the first televised presidential debate between John Kennedy and Richard Nixon was six years away. This was new, uncharted territory for everyone.

The debate was scheduled for nine in the evening. About eight, after a dinner meeting with Harold and Roy, I went down to the hotel lobby to get a "bulldog" edition of the next morning's

Miami Herald. A bulldog edition was a copy of the next day's paper issued the evening before. One article caught my eye. It was an interview with Charley from earlier "that day." It quoted Charley discussing the debate in the past tense. Charley was quoted as saying that he had not only trounced his opponent "last night," but "run Roy Collins right out of town."

I rushed up to Roy's room and spread the newspaper out for everyone to see that "Roy had already lost." Roy tore out the article and stuck it in his pocket, and headed to the television station.

We were seated in a small alcove to one side of the studio. Opposite us, in an identical alcove, was Charley's staff. Between us was a table with Ralph Renick, the commentator, sitting between the candidates. The only other people in the room were the camera crew.

Renick began the program by introducing the candidates and the rules of the debate. He was going to begin by asking a question of Governor Johns, but Roy interrupted him. "Excuse me just a moment, Ralph. There's something I must say." He pulled the paper from his pocket, read the headline and the first paragraph, and concluded by saying, "Charley, I'm looking forward to watching you run me out of town."

Charley was as stunned as a bull hit by an ax. His credibility was shattered. He never regained his composure. Roy won the debate hands down. He beat Charley in the primary, then easily won the general election. Roy was later reelected for a full term as governor in 1956. He was an excellent man and proved a wonderful governor for the state of Florida.

After the election, I went back to practicing law, grateful for the connections I'd made during the campaign. I was correct in thinking that getting out in the community was a good way to attract new clients. This was important, because it took a lot of clients to support three lawyers.

I didn't always handle client relations well. We had one client, a builder, whom I simply could not tolerate. It was the era of anti-Communism fervor, and one day, I could hear him giving Dick an earful about Communist infiltrators. "Thank God for Senator McCarthy, " he said, "because he's going to save us from the Red Scare."

I walked into the office. "That's total B.S.," I declared. "And it's just plain ignorance. Our country is not full of Communists. It's just a horse that Senator McCarthy intends to whip to death."

Not surprisingly, the firm lost that client. Dick and Hardy, however, were forgiving. They agreed that the witch hunts conducted by Senator Joe McCarthy's Senate Government Operations Committee and by the House Un-American Activities Committee were an unprecedented low point in American politics.

Shortly after Roy Collins took office as governor, I got a call from the chairman of the Florida State Turnpike Authority, who told me he wanted me to be the authority's general counsel. I had not sought that or any job as a result of my campaign efforts, but I was certainly happy to get it. The position paid $15,000 a year and didn't require me to give up my law practice. Being general counsel took about half my time, and I spent the rest practicing law.

The Turnpike Authority was created by the Florida legislature to build an arterial highway system connecting Florida's population centers. Legislation provided the Authority the right of eminent domain, the right to charge tolls, and the right to issue revenue bonds to be repaid by the tolls. The five members of the board of directors, appointed by the governor, were competent and excellent to work with.

The first segment of the turnpike was to extend ninety-two miles from Miami north to Fort Pierce. Two engineering firms were hired, one to design the turnpike and another to conduct a financial feasibility study. Our financial consultant, a major Wall Street investment house, projected that the first ninety-two-mile segment would require $72 million in bonds. Under their direction, I created and took our "dog-and-pony" show to New York, Boston, and Chicago to pitch the bonds to investment firms and brokerage offices. We obviously did a good job of selling, because the bonds sold quickly. Our financial estimates proved accurate. The bonds were repaid without difficulty.

One big challenge I faced as general counsel was getting highway engineers to understand that some things are mightier than the bulldozer. South Florida is as flat as a pancake, so the engineering firm designed the highway in a straight line. That meant, however, putting the turnpike through the middle of an old cemetery. I explained to them that Florida law required us to convince a court that we had obtained the written permission of every living descendant of every person whose grave needed to be moved. Such would be a costly, time-consuming, and indeed, impossible task. The engineers wouldn't hear of it. They were too in love with their linear straightaway to consider altering the route. I finally had to enlist the support of Tom Manuel, who was the chairman of the Authority board. Subsequently, the engineers added a gentle curve going around the cemetery.

Life was good. My law practice was growing. I was enjoying the work at the Turnpike Authority. Flavil was happy teaching. And Mark was doing well in school. Our house, though small, was adequate for the moment, and we were able to afford both a telephone and a new car. I was finally making a good living.

I had been at the Turnpike Authority about six months when Governor Collins called, asking me to fill a vacancy at the Railroad and Public Utilities Commission. I respectfully told the governor that I was honored, but I was enjoying my work at the Turnpike Authority and at my law practice.

Roy would not be denied. "Alan, I cannot believe you worked so hard to get me elected and then turn your back on me once I'm in office."

There was, I thought, but one response: "Roy, I'm honored. And I'll take the position if you appoint me."

"I'll appoint you tomorrow, Alan. You will find this position very interesting."

The Florida Railroad and Public Utilities Commission comprised three members, each elected by statewide vote to a four-year term. I was appointed to fill a vacant term expiring at the end of the following year. Roy was correct. I did find the commission's work interesting.

The commission regulated the rates and services of utilities. These included telephone and electric service, as well as surface transportation such as buses, trucks, railroads, barges, and pipelines. We held hearings throughout the state and at our headquarters in Tallahassee. In addition to enjoying my work, traveling around the state made it possible to enlarge my political contacts. It occurred to me that if enough people in Florida came to know me, they couldn't help but develop an irrepressible desire to elect me governor of the state.

When my appointed term was ending, I decided to run for election for a full term as commissioner. This was for two reasons: first, to validate Roy's decision to appoint me; second, to pursue my budding political ambitions.

Although I was running for statewide election, the race for utility commissioner was about as exciting as a race to elect a county dogcatcher. I won by a wide margin, and my new term, which began in 1957, coincided with becoming chairman of the commission for the next two years. Because of the added responsibilities, I decided to close my law practice. I was sad to professionally part with Hardy and Dick, because they had been excellent partners. We continued being dear friends.

Shortly after my election, Senator Smathers called. He and Spessard Holland, Florida's senior senator, wanted to urge President Dwight Eisenhower to nominate me to fill a vacancy on the Civil Aeronautics Board where I had applied to be a lawyer ten years before. I told George that I was honored by the suggestion, but that having just been elected to office, I couldn't let my electorate down by leaving just as my term was beginning. I didn't say that I hoped someday Florida might be fortunate enough to have me as its governor. George wasn't happy, but he accepted my reasoning.

As chairman of the commission, my routine was to fly from Miami to Tallahassee on Mondays, where I stayed with a friend in his two-bedroom apartment. On Thursdays I would fly home to Miami. I use the word *routine* loosely, because every week was different.

The commission was a good place for a governor-in-training. It opened my eyes to bureaucratic politics. I hoped that my commission work would build my reputation in the state, so I was pleased, and utterly surprised, when the Junior Chamber of Commerce named me one of Florida's Five Outstanding Young Men of 1958. Emboldened by the recognition, I broached the subject of a run for governor with a few influential people. I got the same reaction from every one of them: "You would be a great governor, Alan—when you grow up. Come back then and we'll support you." Flavil wasn't much impressed either. I thought I'd make an excellent governor, but disheartened by the lack of enthusiasm I'd encountered, I became disillusioned with politics at the ripe old age of thirty-five. I gave up before I even got started.

Once my term as chairman of the commission expired in January 1959, I was primarily occupied in my commission work by routine matters of rates and service. Occasionally, I spoke to civic groups or lectured to university students about public utility law. The work was pleasant enough, but I was reminded of a rail clerk I'd met in a Jacksonville freight office. He was one of twelve clerks in the office, each with his own identical desk. I had gone around shaking hands and introducing myself.

"Commissioner Boyd," one said proudly, "I've had this same job at *this* desk for forty years."

I congratulated him. I understood he was happy, but—*oh, my God*—that would have been a prison sentence for me. Realizing the Utilities Commission was no longer a challenge, I planned to return to the practice of law when my term expired.

Late in the summer 1959, Senator Smathers called again. "There's another vacancy, Alan, on the Civil Aeronautics Board," he said, "and we want you to fill it. This train is not going to stop at your station many more times," he added for emphasis.

Though I was honored, I told George I needed to talk it over with Flavil. We were happy with our lives in Miami. A few years earlier, we'd sold the house that we had built ourselves and hired a contractor to build a new three-bedroom home. The new house was on a cul-de-sac closer to town, with many other young families as neighbors. Flavil had her work, and Mark had his friends, and he'd be starting high school the following year.

When I told her about the job with the CAB, Flavil was reluctant. She didn't know a soul in Washington. Still, she agreed to the move. I called George the next day and told him yes.

XII

Washington

A few days later I received a phone call. "Mr. Boyd, my name is David Kendall. I am special counsel to President Eisenhower. He was wondering if you would have time to stop by the White House for a talk."

I was humored that my first thought was that *of course* I could find space in my calendar to visit the White House. A few weeks later I flew to Washington and met David. We later became dear friends. David didn't take me to meet the president. Instead I was shown into the office of General Wilton Persons, Eisenhower's chief of staff.

Sitting in the general's office in the West Wing looking out the window at the old Executive Office Building across the parking lot, the memory of my unplanned flight over the White House came to mind. I hoped my reception on this visit would be better.

I had a nice conversation with the general about my experience as a pilot and as a lawyer. We talked about my family. After about twenty minutes, the conversation began to wind down. General Persons straightened up in his chair and looked at me intently. "Mr. Boyd, I have one final question for you. Do you believe in private enterprise?"

I was speechless for a moment, wondering what Republicans must think it means to be a Democrat. I maintained my composure. "General, not only do I believe in private enterprise, but I am a firm believer in the profit motive."

The general stood up, put his hand across the desk, and shook my hand. "Mr. Boyd, it's a pleasure to meet you. You will be hearing from us shortly."

About ten days later, I was notified that President Eisenhower had sent my name to the Senate as a nominee to fill a vacancy on the Civil Aeronautics Board.

Congress created the five-member Civil Aeronautics Board with the 1938 Civil Aeronautics Act, which basically declared that airlines were public utilities and needed to be regulated. The board's mission was to see that the airlines served the maximum number of people with the best possible service at a fair price while allowing the airlines to earn a reasonable profit. The board controlled the establishment of routes for scheduled airlines, both domestically and internationally (for US flag carriers). It reviewed and approved or disapproved proposed fares by the airlines. It also dispersed subsidies to support flights on routes that would not be economically viable without government support. These were usually routes to smaller cities that wouldn't garner service without subsidies.

The board also did economic analysis on air routes and functioned with the State Department in negotiating air traffic rights with other nations. It was responsible for investigating aviation accidents and making safety recommendations to the industry.

My confirmation hearing before the Senate Commerce Committee was without excitement or incident. Both Florida senators accompanied me to the hearing and, very kindly, expressed superlatives about my knowledge, my qualities, and my character. The committee members then asked about my background as a pilot and as a lawyer, and about my experience as a utility regulator. I was unanimously confirmed. On November 17, 1959, I was duly sworn in as a member of the US Civil Aeronautics Board.

My fellow board members were congenial, knowledgeable people. We became good friends. My transition onto the board was smooth, thanks to my fellow members and the staff of the CAB, which was made up of some of the best professionals I have ever known in government or in business. They were a superb, professional group.

I called Dean Ribble of the University of Virginia law school and asked him to recommend an assistant for me. He suggested Charles Biondi, a graduate of the law school, who had worked for Philippine Airlines as well as the International Air Transport Association, the governing organization for all airlines that flew international routes. Charles agreed to join me, which was one of the great good fortunes of my very fortunate life.

Charles was brilliant. He spoke several languages, loved music and art, and was a shrewd judge of character. His humor and his laugh were infectious. He had an enormous store of knowledge about aviation as well as many other things. He was very cultured and engaging, and had a sincere desire to be helpful to everyone in the organization. It didn't take him long to become friends with everybody on staff, especially the other four board assistants.

When I was at the Florida Railroad and Public Utilities Commission, I learned that one's staff is a powerful and essential part of the decision-making process. It was the staff who intimately knew what was going on and got things done.

I knew the same thing would apply in Washington. Senators and congressmen spent much of their time horse-trading and taking care of their constituents' problems. I walked with George Smathers from his office to the Capitol on several occasions while his chief of staff briefed him about what he was going to vote on and how he should vote. It wasn't that George couldn't figure it out himself, but he had so much to do that he relied on his staff to help him stay on top of things. I told friends and colleagues coming to Washington that it's the staffers you want and need to know. Take them to lunch. Show them the respect they deserve. They're fierce gatekeepers, but they can also be great friends and allies.

My assistant, Charles, was a good example. When something needed to be decided, the board would hear arguments from counsel for the different sides of the issue. A few weeks later the board would hold a private conference to discuss our views and positions. Charles was always able to tell me the concerns of the other board members and how they planned to vote. He was of invaluable assistance to me, particularly after I became chairman.

Shortly after I was sworn in as a member of the board, Juan Trippe, founder of Pan American World Airways, called to say he wanted to meet me. Pan American was the United States' largest international carrier and the first to use jets for passenger service. Mr. Trippe was influential. He was a friend of the president and of other important people in Washington, as well as many in foreign governments. He asked my secretary for an early morning appointment.

On the morning of the appointed day, I arrived at my office about 8:00 a.m. A gentleman was talking to my secretary. I said hello and went on into my private office. My secretary showed

Mr. Trippe in. Most visitors sat in the comfortable armchair in front of my desk, but he chose to sit in the simple wooden chair at the side of my desk, the one my secretary used when taking dictation. He put his little briefcase on his lap, set his hat on top of it, and looked up at me intently.

"Mr. Boyd," he said in a soft voice, "I just wanted to meet my new boss," meaning, of course, that as a member of the CAB, I had considerable say in what happened in American and international aviation.

My immediate thought was, "Zip up your pockets. Here is a con man if I ever saw one."

We had a cordial conversation of no consequence. I thanked him for coming. Later, I would get to know Juan, and I liked him. But I never did trust him. Yet he was brilliant and did a fantastic job of developing Pan American into the world's premier airline.

I had been in Washington only about three weeks when my secretary told me that Flavil and I were invited to an aviation reception at Blair House, the official presidential guesthouse, where visiting foreign leaders and dignitaries stayed. We had both read about the historic home built in 1824. Flavil and I were somewhat agog at the thought of visiting it.

We entered the reception room and noticed that, other than the waitstaff, Flavil was the only woman there. Obviously there'd been a communication mix-up with my office. I suggested that if she put on an apron and started serving drinks, she would fit right in. She did not find my humor amusing.

A few minutes later, Pete Quesada, a retired Air Force general and the Federal Aviation administrator, arrived with his wife. It turned out to be a very pleasant evening and a great way to strengthen the bonds between the CAB and the Federal Aviation Agency. Blair House was worth the visit.

One of the important, interesting, and lengthy cases the board dealt with was the Southern Transcontinental Route case. I came onto the board during the final stages of the case. Routes from cities such as Miami and Atlanta to West Coast cities such as San Francisco and Los Angeles were being assigned. All the major airlines wanted the routes. An extensive body of argument and evidence had been submitted. Louis Hector, the man I succeeded on the CAB, was an old friend of mine, a fellow lawyer from Miami. He took me into his office and showed me the fifteen feet of files he had on the case, all lined up along the wall.

On the opening day of final arguments, at least a dozen members of the House and Senate were scheduled to appear to argue on behalf of their various constituent cities. None offered anything that hadn't already been hashed or rehashed. Nevertheless, that didn't stop them from taking up half a day of board time.

Eastern Airlines wanted the routes, and started their argument by seating their CEO, Captain Eddie Rickenbacker, in the front row of the spectators' seats. Rickenbacker had been America's greatest flying ace in World War I. As a civilian during WWII, he was on a mission in the Pacific for President Roosevelt when his plane crashed. Amazingly, and heroically, he survived twenty-four days at sea on a raft. Eastern's lawyer made no effort to present the merits of their application.

Instead, he used his allotted time to extol Captain Eddie's heroism and service to his country. He ended his argument by saying prayerfully, almost tearfully, that the only recognition that Captain Eddie wanted after all his heroic efforts for his country was the chance for Eastern Airlines to fly from Miami to the West Coast.

That was, from the perspective of the board, a really disastrous argument. Unfortunately for Eastern, it failed to land successfully.

Flavil and Mark moved to Washington in December 1959, at the end of their school semester. We had quite an adjustment to make, moving from a three-bedroom house on a quiet cul-de-sac to a two-bedroom apartment on the fourth floor of a building on busy Connecticut Avenue. But the location was convenient. I could take a bus to my office, which was also on Connecticut Avenue. And Mark could walk a few blocks to his new school.

Flavil, wanting to be free to travel with me and keep an eye on Mark, quit teaching. Deciding to learn Spanish, she posted a notice on the bulletin board at Mark's school, looking for a Spanish-speaking parent who could teach her Spanish in return for English lessons. Magi Imposti responded. Magi's husband, Rudi, was the Argentine naval attaché and her son Felix was in Mark's class.

Magi was one of the nicest people I have ever known. She played the guitar like a professional and had a voice that could make Joan Baez jealous. Flavil realized that learning to play the guitar was more fun than learning Spanish, so Magi gave Flavil guitar lessons in exchange for Flavil helping Magi with her English. Our families became good friends. They gave us a deep appreciation for the Latin people and music. They even invited Mark to live with them in Buenos Aires one summer. Flavil and I found Washington to be full of wonderful, interesting people.

One of the responsibilities of the CAB was involvement with international aviation. The government of Singapore invited me to their first-ever air show in 1960. In the process of attending, I learned the rigors of international air travel firsthand. I flew from Washington to New York, and changed planes for Seattle. Then I caught a flight to Tokyo—that had a stopover in Anchorage. In Tokyo, I caught a plane to Hong Kong, and from there, I finally flew on to Singapore. I arrived about two in the morning. I was so tired, I didn't know day from night.

I was driven to a government guesthouse, the residence of the British governor before WWII. I settled into a nice suite with a living area and a bedroom. The living room was air-conditioned. But the air-conditioning unit, installed over the door to the bedroom, vented hot exhaust into the room where I was to sleep. That first night it didn't matter: I slept the sleep of the dead.

On the last night of my stay, Singapore's prime minister hosted a dinner for all invited foreign representatives. Other than two British members of Parliament and myself, all the other guests were from Asian countries that had been part of the British Empire. They all made angry speeches directed at the English, excoriating them for the "plunder and pillage" their countries had endured during the British Colonial period. The members of Parliament stayed calm and polite, furthering my respect of the British. I noticed that the prime minister, Lee Kuan Yew, the founding father of modern Singapore, smiled benignly, obviously enjoying the performance. I sensed it was a good time for me to remain silent.

I occasionally participated as part of the US delegation that negotiated with other countries in an effort to gain more routes for our international carriers, including Pan American, TWA, Northwest, and Braniff. The US airlines were efficient, profit-driven enterprises, but many of the foreign airlines served as a government jobs program, providing good-paying jobs for skilled workers. These airlines were owned either directly or indirectly by their governments. That made them less focused on profit, and inefficient relative to the US carriers. British Airways, for example, had several employees doing the same function as one Pan Am employee.

Many countries would have been happy to let US carriers fly in and out of their airports without limitation. The caveat, however, was that they wanted 50 percent of all the revenues generated on those routes—regardless of which airline generated it. The US carriers, as private businesses, of course, needed to keep their profits. They wanted permission to fly in and out of a country as often as economically feasible.

In negotiating international air treaty rights, there are what are referred to as "the six freedoms of the air." The first freedom is the right to fly over a country. The second, which is rarely used anymore, is the right to stop for refueling or do maintenance in a country. The third is the right to fly from my country to your country, and the fourth is the ability to fly from your country to my country. The fifth is to fly from my country to your country, pick up passengers, and then fly to a third country. The sixth— the ultimate freedom—is having unrestricted access, thereby creating "open skies" for each participating country.

The fifth freedom proved a major issue in our negotiations with India. US airlines wanted to pick up passengers in India as they were in transit to other places, such as Singapore. The Indian government insisted on receiving 50 percent of all airline revenues, which was unacceptable to us.

We started negotiations in Delhi and continued in Washington. It was a frustrating activity. Indian bureaucracy, trained by the British, seemed to love acquiring reams of documents that they held together with string. Most of them seemed irrelevant, in my opinion. Our discussions were lengthy. In the end, they did not get 50 percent of the revenues they wanted, and our airlines gained only a few of the routes they'd desired.

Even though many negotiations with other countries were challenging, the people involved were typically delightful. I was in Rome once, engaged in a debate with the Italians, who wanted a fifty percent revenue split. I was pontificating about the virtues of free-market competition when my Italian counterpart, the director general of Civil Aviation, interrupted me.

"Alan," he said in his charming accent, "there was an old Roman poet named Tasso, who once said, 'If you have a chicken and I have none, on balance we each have half a chicken. But I am still hungry!'"

Later that same trip, I was trying to peel a peach for dessert. The Italian waiter, seeing my struggle, came over to elegantly and easily remove the skin. I asked him to teach me the technique. At lunch a few days later my friend Najeeb "Jeeb" Halaby was struggling with a peach. I reached over, took it from him, and said graciously, "Allow me, Jeeb." With a few waves of my hand, I released his peach from its skin. The next day, a beautiful alabaster peach arrived in my hotel room. The enclosed note read, "Peel this, you S.O.B.! Jeeb."

My assistant, Charles, had some wonderful stories about what he witnessed when he worked with the International Air Transport Association, such as negotiations over what beverages could be provided for free on international routes. The French, naturally, wanted to promote French wine and serve it for free. American carriers didn't have access to wine but had access to Coca-Cola, which they wanted to serve for free. After many hours of stalemate, the French returned from a break to announce that everything was resolved. French airlines would provide free Coca-Cola bottles, "but in those Coca-Cola bottles there will be wine."

My first term on the CAB ended in December 1960. President Kennedy then nominated me for a six-year term as chairman. I assume George Smathers influenced Kennedy, a close personal friend, to elevate me to chairman. Smathers had been a groomsman at Kennedy's wedding.

One of the first policy regulation changes I proposed as chairman was to allow only counsel of record to present evidence or arguments to the board. Board decisions were essentially a judicial process. With the Transcontinental Southern Route case in mind, I wanted to reduce the amount of wasted board and staff time. Listening to congressmen and senators repeat information that had already been presented by legal counsel was a waste of everybody's time.

My Democratic colleagues opposed it, but the two Republicans on the board supported me, and we passed the rule change. Under the Administrative Procedures Act, we were required to publicize a copy of the new regulation sixty days before it became effective. If no comment was presented in opposition, the regulation would go into effect. I made sure that every senator and every member of Congress received a copy of the draft regulation by mail. There was no response, so the regulation quietly went into effect.

Later, when another hearing was scheduled, a member of Congress asked to be put on the calendar to speak. The board clerk replied that only counsel of record could do so. A holy uproar ensued.

I was hauled before a subcommittee of the House Interstate and Foreign Commerce Committee, chaired by Congressman John Moss of California. Paul Rogers, a congressman from Florida—a friend of mine since college—was also a member on the subcommittee.

Chairman Moss and other subcommittee members "walked up and down my back," asking, "Who do you think you are, telling Congress what it can and cannot do?" They pointed out that the CAB was a creature of Congress, and that Congress could do with the board as it pleased. My friend Paul sat and laughed at me silently.

My response was simple. "Gentlemen, the Civil Aeronautics Board is a creature of Congress. Congress designated the board as a judicial body to adjudicate aviation law. I'm sure you know that only counsel of record are allowed to present in a court of law. If you gentlemen feel that you are entitled to a double standard because you are members of Congress, and you want to specify in legislation that you shall be entitled to appear before the board whenever you wish, that is your prerogative. I'm not sure the public would understand that double standard, but that is up to you."

Everyone knew the new regulation was in their best interest. It would save all of us time and energy. But that didn't stop them from venting their spleen and making a show of it. I knew I was on solid ground, so I rather enjoyed the banter.

When it was over, I went up to greet Paul. As I walked past a congressman from Michigan, he slapped me on the back. "Don't take it too seriously, Alan," he said. "It's nothing personal."

At lunch, Paul gleefully remarked that I'd provided him with the best laugh he'd had in a long time. To my delight, the new policy stood.

As chairman of the CAB, I testified every year before a subcommittee of the House Appropriations Committee to explain our proposed budget. The biggest expenditure was subsidies to airlines, which were mandated by Congress but allocated by the CAB. Subsidies were used to support small carriers on routes that couldn't generate enough revenue to sustain them yet were deemed important to the economic health of the communities they served.

Since Congress appropriated the money for this, my testimony was usually a routine matter. An exception was in 1962. Congressman Albert Thomas of Texas was chairman of the subcommittee that year. He was a fiscal conservative who had a jaundiced view of subsidies. He made negative remarks as I went through my statement. He asked me why the local service carriers should be getting subsidies.

I went through the drill of why Congress had approved subsidies. As I continued with my presentation, he kept coming back to the subsidies, making negative comments about them and repeatedly asking me to explain why Congress should make such appropriations.

I went through my song and dance one more time, then proceeded to other aspects of our budget. When he came back to the subsidy issue again, asking me to explain it, I lost my temper. I remember thinking I was always at liberty to leave the CAB. "I don't have to put up with this crap," I thought. "And I'm not going to sit here and be treated in this fashion."

I said something to the effect of, "Mr. Chairman, for the third time, I am going to explain to you the reason for the subsidy request. I am going to do it in a fashion that would be understood by a sixth grader, and I want to start with A, B, C. *A* is for airline. *B* is for business. *C* is for community."

At that moment the gavel came down sharply. He declared a recess, stood up, and walked out. I went out into the hall fuming. After pacing up and down for a few minutes, trying to cool off, one of the congressman's assistants, whom I knew and liked, came over to me.

"You shouldn't talk to the chairman that way, Alan. He knows he went beyond being reasonable. The two of you need to get together and make up so that we can go on with this hearing."

I went into where the chairman was sitting. I apologized and told him I knew I had lost my temper. I hoped he would understand and pardon me.

"Alan, I don't like subsidies," he said, "but I know that you're not the one responsible for them. I went overboard. I should not have badgered you the way I did, and I, too, apologize."

We had a cordial rest of the hearing. Interestingly, Congressman Thomas and I became very good friends for the balance of my time in the government.

Another critical function of the CAB was to investigate all aviation accidents involving US flag carriers, all accidents on US soil, and all accidents involving American-manufactured aircraft. The purpose was to establish probable cause. Each accident was assigned on a rotating basis to a member of the board. The detail work was done by our outstanding staff of experts who, without exception, were extremely competent professionals dedicated to making aviation as safe as possible.

One case I was assigned was the crash of a twin-engine Convair CV-240 owned by Vice President Lyndon Johnson's ranch. On a night in bad weather, the plane crashed into a hillside near the ranch. The plane's occupants, the pilot and copilot, were both killed.

I had met then–Senator Johnson previously in 1958 when I was chairman of the Florida Railroad and Public Utilities Commission. He made a visit to Florida to gauge support for a possible presidential campaign. George Smathers, a good friend of Johnson's, introduced us. We had a short, pleasant conversation. I was impressed by the man.

Once assigned the accident investigation, I became well acquainted with Vice President Johnson. Even though he was very busy, he was on the telephone every day wanting to know what we had found. His concern seemed to be for the families of the crew. He wanted nothing to negatively affect the insurance payout to the families of the pilot and copilot.

The investigation took months, which was normal. The investigators were careful and verified every fact with two independent sources. In our many conversations, Johnson asked cogent questions and never wasted his time or mine, though on occasion, we did get off topic. I never told my investigators that the vice president was phoning me every day. He never tried to influence me, the investigation, or the statement of probable cause in any way. Our rapport was easy and respectful. In the end, the cause of the accident was determined to be severe weather.

In the early 1960s, the airline industry transitioned from propeller-driven planes to jets. Boeing's 707, the first American passenger jet, used less and cheaper fuel, carried more passengers, and required less maintenance than a propeller-driven plane. I believed such reductions in cost should be passed on to the consumer on flights within the country, where the CAB regulated rates. International rates were more complicated.

The International Air Transport Association (IATA) was basically a monopoly trade organization made up of all the international airlines, except those in the Soviet bloc. IATA met annually to set international airfares. Those airfares had to be approved by the unanimous vote of IATA members. Pan Am, TWA, Northwest, and Braniff were members and were allowed to participate in IATA's monopoly, with immunity from anti-trust prosecution as long as they voted as instructed by the CAB.

For the 1962 IATA meeting, the CAB instructed the US carriers that international airfares needed to be reduced substantially to reflect the economics of the new jets. Instead, IATA voted unanimously for some increased rates. The CAB called representatives of our carriers in and asked them what the hell was going on. They claimed that they had failed to find allies for lowering rates, and that they were threatened with dire consequences from several countries if they didn't agree to the new rates. Since most of the member airlines were government owned, these threats were genuine.

Dissatisfied with this, the Civil Aeronautics Board disapproved the international fares, effectively scuttling the agreement on international rates. This created a situation of "open rates"—where airlines were free to charge the fares they thought costs dictated.

US carriers lowered their rates. Other members of IATA were not happy with our veto and fought back. When a Pan American flight landed in Stockholm, the Swedish government required every passenger to pay the difference between the lower Pan Am airfare and the IATA rate before allowing them to get off the plane. The British minister of aviation was so upset that he threatened to confiscate US planes landing in London. US carriers began making arrangements to land in Holland in case that happened.

The British Aviation Ministry called a meeting in London for aviation authorities from the United States, Canada, Australia, and France. I went with the US delegation and set up office in the American Embassy. Meeting with representatives from the other countries, I found Canada to be our only ally. The rest remained opposed to my stance that savings stemming from the use of jets should be passed on to the passengers. The other parties were not swayed by my argument that lower airfares would encourage more passengers and improve revenues.

Each day after negotiations, I would send a wire to inform the State Department and the White House on the progress of negotiations. I also held a daily press conference at the American Embassy.

I excoriated the other governments for their refusal to reduce the cost of air travel for the public. I pointed out their callous disregard for the interests of their own citizens. The press conferences got a lot of attention in the British press.

In one press announcement, I said, "We are in London, the home of the British Empire. Yet with the improvements possible because of modern jet airplanes, the British government is working against its own citizens by making air travel more expensive and discouraging Americans from flying to Britain to spend their tourism dollars."

This continued for several days and played well with the British media, which gave my press conferences quite a bit of coverage. I admit I enjoyed the publicity.

After days of vitriolic discussion without any progress, and because of the publicity my press conferences were generating, the American ambassador received a call from Washington. He informed me that President Kennedy wanted me to return to Washington immediately and visit him in the White House.

I caught the next plane and arrived at the White House about eight in the evening. I was ushered into the cabinet room. President Kennedy was sitting at the large rectangular table, going over papers with Secretary of State Dean Rusk.

Without preamble, President Kennedy said, "What the hell do you think you're doing in England? The prime minister called me and indicated that your actions are creating great embarrassment for the British government. The British are our close friends. I want you to go back and tell the British that the US agrees with the position they have taken."

His comments angered me. I had sent wires every day to both the State Department and the White House, reporting what I was doing and what I was planning to do. It seemed clear to me that neither of the two men in the cabinet room had received the information until they heard about it from Harold Macmillan, the prime minister of England. It also occurred to me that this was no time to talk to them about the failure of communication within their organizations. It was clear the president wanted the situation resolved.

"Yes sir," I said, and left.

I returned on the next flight to London and said that our position had changed and that we would accept the fares as they had been voted by IATA. Before doing so, however, I got a commitment that there would be another IATA meeting to discuss fares within six months and that I would expect the fares to be more reflective of the new reality of jet travel costs. Within a few months, airfares began to come down. I like to think that the assertions I made in the media may have helped make that happen.

In the 1960s, the regulated aviation industry was still fairly small. There were no more than ten so-called "trunk" airlines operating between major cities, and only two all-cargo carriers in operation. Within two years of my arrival at the board, I had gotten to know the major players in the industry. By 1965, I had been at the board for about five years, and though I thoroughly enjoyed every aspect of the job, the issues the board dealt with had begun to become repetitive. I began to question the need for the CAB as the airline industry matured. I thought the airlines no longer needed to be considered a regulated utility, and that the public might be better served through free-market competition. I didn't like that routes were assigned arbitrarily. Though the board offered reasons why one airline was awarded a route over other carriers, there were no established, objective guidelines. The CAB's only essential function was accident investigation, which could be transferred to another agency. I loved the people of the CAB and enjoyed the industry, but I felt the need for another challenge.

Flavil and I were enjoying life in Washington. It was a friendly place in the late fifties and early sixties. Many members of Congress brought their families to Washington. Their children attended school together, and their wives joined clubs and shared activities. Members of Congress were more likely to play golf or bridge together on weekends than to head home to campaign.

I think part of the reason was that air travel was still somewhat difficult. It was not easy to make quick weekend trips to every part of the country. As a result, members of Congress were friends and neighbors. They were cordial to each other. There were never any personal attacks or insinuations about members of the other party. Every state had an association where its entire congressional delegation, both houses of Congress and members of both parties, would have gatherings, often at a senator's or congressman's home. It was often a dinner with spouses and kids invited. Some would cluster around a piano and sing. These social events fostered constructive, personal connections.

Even the leaders of the parties were pleasant with each other. One of my favorite stories, which may be more legend than fact, involved LBJ when he was Senate majority leader, and Everett Dirksen, then Senate minority leader.

One day Dirksen received a phone call from Lyndon.

"Hello, Ev," Johnson said. "I'm calling you from the phone in my car. I thought you might like to know how to reach me if you need to."

Dirksen had never heard of a car phone. But he, as the story was told, had to have one if Johnson did.

A week later Johnson answered the phone in his car.

"Hello, Lyndon, this is Everett. I'm calling you from the phone in my car."

"Hold on just a minute, will you, Ev," replied Lyndon without missing a beat. "My other phone is ringing."

Having decided it was time for a new challenge, I was considering returning to Miami and the practice of law. I called John Macy, chairman of the Civil Service Commission. We'd become good friends over the years. He and I used to meet with our counterparts at the Federal Maritime Commission and at the Interstate Commerce Commission to talk about our agencies, to share notes on how we did things, and to try to learn what worked and what didn't. It was our own informal administrator support group. John also served as President Johnson's executive recruiter. I asked John to meet me for lunch.

I told him how much I enjoyed living in Washington, working in the government, and having had the opportunity to serve as chairman of the CAB. I told him my thoughts about returning to Miami, but said I wanted to give the president time to find a good successor for me.

John asked if I would be interested in any other position in the government.

"Yes, I would, if the position appealed to me."

"Don't do anything until you hear from me, Alan," John said.

About two months later came the phone call from Jim Jones at the White House that interrupted my lunch at the Metropolitan Club. I rushed to the White House for the surprise announcement that I was to become undersecretary of commerce for transportation. I couldn't wait to get home and tell Flavil about it.

Before I told my news, Flavil told me that she had had quite a surprising and interesting day that she wished to share. Lady Bird Johnson had called her shortly after I left for work to say she was having a few of her friends over for lunch at the White House and would be honored if Flavil would join her. Of course Flavil had accepted, and lunch was very pleasant. Just as they were finishing, Lady Bird told Flavil there was an interesting television program on at the moment that she thought Flavil would like to watch. She led Flavil into the Lincoln Bedroom and turned on the television. Fascinated, Flavil watched the news conference that was occurring almost directly beneath her. Needless to say, Flavil learned my exciting news at the same time I did. Both the president and Lady Bird were full of surprises.

XIII

A Coherent Transportation System

My nomination as under secretary was confirmed by the Senate without dissent. I took office in the Commerce Department, under the aegis of Secretary of Commerce John T. Connor. I thought highly of Jack. He was a lovely man, a very fine organizer, and an excellent leader. When we faced a challenging issue, Jack would say, "Let's just walk all the way around this," then lead us through an examination of the problem.

Franklin D. Roosevelt Jr. was the other under secretary of commerce. Jack and Frank were welcoming, and I immediately felt at home.

Life became exciting in a hurry. Three weeks after I arrived, the Seafarers International Union (SIU) led a strike on US flagged ships, ships registered in the United States. The White House looked to me for advice on how to deal with the strike. With my previous regulatory experience, I was knowledgeable about air and land transportation, but I didn't know stem from stern about shipping. But I discovered that the Department of Commerce had a senior civil servant expert in maritime issues whose job it was to assist the under secretary on maritime issues. I asked him to provide me with background information and advice on the strike.

He shocked me by saying, "My job is only to tell you facts. That's all I will do."

I was astonished to encounter a very senior government adviser unwilling to do his job. Finding him both oppositional and useless, I replied, "Then get your ass out of my office and never come back."

I also quickly discovered that it takes months and an enormous amount of paperwork to get rid of an incompetent civil servant. I was unable to get rid of him. I'm not proud to say that I left him in an office with no secretary or phone, only a desk.

The strike was resolved in less than two weeks, but I learned in the process that much of the maritime industry was like my so-called senior adviser, wanting money from the government without reciprocal service. Many US shipping companies operated ships identical to—even built from the same blueprints as—ships operated by foreign lines. The Norwegian Maersk Line operated such ships with a crew of twenty. The US flagged ships, however, operated identical vessels with a crew of forty-eight—paid for with subsidies from the US government. As if that was not bad enough, the government also subsidized the construction of US-built ships at nearly three times the cost of identical ships built elsewhere.

Cushioned by government subsidies, the US shipbuilders and shipping companies showed no interest in innovation and efficiency. With few exceptions, I was unimpressed with the management of the US flag carriers. They were, however, very effective at entertaining and contributing to the campaigns of congressional members essential to gaining and maintaining their subsidies. Maritime subsidies had started in the 1930s to create a reserve of able-bodied seamen and ships for national defense in the event of war, an important notion with war imminent in Europe. Thirty years later, the subsidies insulated an inefficient and aging industry from any need to compete.

Federal law required that a ship sailing under a US flag, or sailing from one US port to another, be built in the United States. This created a demand for US ship construction, with the government subsidizing costs exorbitantly higher than ships built in Greece or Japan. With this government largesse, there was absolutely no incentive for US shipbuilders to innovate or become more efficient. For example, US-built ships were put together with rivets, a WWII-based technology, whereas overseas shipbuilders used more efficient and stronger welding techniques.

Some US shipowners did purchase foreign-built ships. They registered them in foreign countries, most commonly Panama and Liberia, and sailed them under so-called "flags of convenience." This enabled them to be more operationally cost-efficient in the competitive international shipping business.

It seemed to me that unions controlled everything from shipbuilding to shipping, including wages and crew size. I am a strong believer in the importance of unions, but my support falls far short of creating unnecessary jobs at government expense. I consulted with Nicholas Johnson, administrator of the Maritime Administration. Though Nick was new to maritime issues, he was very bright. After talking to him and a number of other people in whom I had confidence, I concluded that both the construction and operating subsidies were a waste of taxpayer money. Additionally they were contrary to enhancing the health and efficiency of our shipping industry.

I made an appointment with President Johnson to propose a change. Entering the Oval Office, I found the president with his new special assistant for domestic affairs, Joseph Califano. Joe was a brilliant young man who'd previously been at the Defense

Department. This was his first week with the president. Joe sat on the sofa, taking notes on our conversation. The president prowled around the office, fiddling with objects as I followed him, outlining my views. I knew LBJ was tracking every word. Finally he stopped and turned.

"You don't know what you're talking about, Alan," he said. "The merchant marine is our fourth arm of defense. If we got into another war without it, we would be totally helpless."

"The Fourth Arm of Defense" was the label the shipping industry and the American Legion had used effectively as propaganda around Washington.

"Mr. President," I said, "you are crazy as hell."

Joe seemed shocked that I would address the president in such a tone. But I had gotten to know the president, and knew he would take my comments in stride. I pointed out that American shipping companies owned hundreds of ships registered under flags of convenience. Those ships had served the United States during WWII and Korea, and they would be available in case of future need.

"All right, you bastard," the president shot back. "I know you're right. And I also know you're going to get us both killed politically. I'll support you for a year. See what you can do." He said he knew I was seeking to do the right thing for the country, and hoped that I could make it happen.

The path to ending subsidies, I knew, was legislation. Legislation starts with congressional committees. If I couldn't get the issue introduced and discussed in committee, it was dead. I tried to find a representative who would support my cause. A lot of "horse-trading" goes on in Congress. When you want to cut something that's a "goody," the first thing a representative thinks is, "Which of my goodies might I have to trade away to get votes?"

I approached my neighbor, a congressman from California who was on the commerce committee. His reaction was typical of the other committee members and staff.

"Don't talk to me, Alan, about rescinding maritime subsidies—because that's an issue that is going to go nowhere."

Word spread about my campaign at the Capitol. Some representatives agreed with my position, though they wouldn't act. Others went to the president to complain.

"He's my boy," the president would tell them, "and he's doing what I asked him to do."

I considered going to the public, as I had in London over airfares, but that would be a direct challenge to the unions, and they'd see to it that I became persona non grata with members of Congress. And without Congress, I couldn't do my job. I decided instead to go directly to the biggest union, the Seafarers International Union of North America, and its powerful president, Paul Hall.

Paul and I knew each other and had a cordial relationship. He was tough. He had grown his union to almost eight million members with hard-nosed tactics and political savvy. And he was the prime mover behind the maritime industry. I met with him three or four times at SIU's headquarters in Brooklyn. Though our meetings were cordial, he wouldn't budge.

"Alan," he told me at one meeting, "I'm going to cut your throat—but it's nothing personal."

His local congressman and close political ally was John Rooney. Congressman Rooney was chairman of the subcommittee of the House Appropriations Committee, before which I routinely had to appear to testify about the transportation portion of the Commerce Department's annual request for appropriations.

Rooney let it be known widely in maritime circles that he would turn me inside out and upside down, and take me apart bone by bone. I knew enough about the congressman to know that he was as mean as a black snake and fully intended to put me through whatever degree of torture he could muster. Needless to say, even though I felt the rightness of my position, I was under great stress because of what could happen at the hearing.

On the appointed day, I was the first witness after lunch. I sat at the witness table with my budget assistant as the subcommittee members wandered in to take their seats. Some of them chatted briefly with the chairman. The ones who knew me nodded a greeting. At 1:00 p.m., Congressman Rooney pounded his gavel to call the hearing to order. He started in with his preamble. As he spoke, the side door opened and in walked the Honorable George Mahon, congressman from West Texas and chairman of the full Appropriations Committee.

As chairman of the full House Appropriations Committee, George was one of the most powerful men in Congress. George was also a very good friend of mine. We had met when Flavil and I moved from our Connecticut Avenue apartment to a building in Rosslyn, Virginia, next to Arlington Cemetery and just behind the Iwo Jima Memorial. Our neighbors, four doors down the hall, were George and Helen Mahon. We spent many Saturday nights together for dinner and bridge. They were two of the sweetest people I've ever known. I had never mentioned to George my situation with Rooney's committee.

Every subcommittee in Congress had a chair on the dais reserved for the full committee chairman, should he care to make an appearance. George strolled into the hearing room, greeting subcommittee members and slapping a few backs as he made his way to his chair. As George sat down, he congenially looked around the room. Finally, his gaze fell on me.

"Well, Alan," he said, "I know you and Flavil beat Helen and me at bridge last Saturday, but we're gonna get you next Saturday night."

He sat there and smiled for a little while, looking around the room, then got up, bowed, and left. George sent a clear message: "Alan Boyd is my friend. Don't touch him." The hearing resumed. Rooney accepted my written statement, asked a few perfunctory questions, and excused me.

It is hard to express the amount of gratitude I felt for George's generous, timely, and public expression of friendship. It did not, however, win the legislative battle for me.

After twelve months of effort, I accepted that maritime subsidies were harder to get rid of than my incompetent civil servant. The system was deeply entrenched. The political forces were too strong. I had other things to do. I went back to the Oval Office and told the president I had failed.

"I knew you would, Alan," the president said. "But you gave it a good try."

My fight to end subsidies was over, but my union troubles continued in the aviation industry. Propeller-driven planes required a cockpit crew of three—pilot, copilot, and a flight engineer or mechanic. Flight engineers had been necessary on planes with internal combustion engines because they required constant attention and adjustment while running. Jet engines, by comparison, are simple pieces of machinery, making flight engineers obsolete. The airlines, in response, offered to retrain flight engineers as pilots to ensure their job security.

The International Association of Machinists (IAM), to whom the flight engineers belonged, chose to insist that flight engineers be continued to be required on jets. To persuade the airlines to their point of view, the IAM threatened an industry-wide strike. An emergency labor board was created to consider the issues and come up with ideas for averting a strike. I was summoned to the White House to share my knowledge and advice.

Though intelligent, from time to time I have still managed to exhibit a considerable amount of stupidity. After meeting with the president in the Oval Office, I walked through the room where the press corps always sat. Someone asked about the meeting. Although one never reveals what the president said, I did share my personal opinion without thought.

"There is no need for flight engineers on jet aircraft. They are about as useful as teats on a boar, and I think Mr. Roy Siemiller, the president of the IAM, must be a Socialist."

It occurred to me on the way back to my office that my utterance was not very politic. Others, it seemed, shared the thought. The White House called and ordered me to return immediately to tell the press I was wrong and apologize. Without reservation, I did as I was told. Although I had honestly expressed my thoughts, I knew my statements had been foolish and were not helpful to a final resolution of the problem.

Another one of my responsibilities was guiding the Highway Beautification legislation through Congress. The Highway Beautification Act, or HBA, was designed to remove the plethora of billboards from major highways, requiring them to be set back at a distance that would be neither an environmental blight nor a safety distraction.

Lady Bird Johnson felt strongly that billboards on interstate highways were eyesores. She appreciated nature and the beauty of the land, and wanted the highways lined with landscaping and wildflowers. I concurred with her about billboards being a distraction to drivers and an automobile safety issue.

The bill was introduced in both houses of Congress—and went nowhere. The billboard interests were very influential with the congressmen and senators in charge of the relevant committees with oversight to the issue. They were so entrenched that I was unable to get a hearing date before the House public works committee to have the bill discussed and acted on. All bills have to be heard in committee before being brought to the House or Senate floor for a vote. The chairman of the House subcommittee on roads, Congressman John Kluczynski of Illinois, controlled what legislation could get a hearing. I called John for two months, trying to get a hearing date. He ignored me.

Then, one evening, I got a call from President Johnson. "Alan, get up to the House tomorrow morning at eight. Go to Kluczynski's office and get a hearing date."

"Mr. President," I said, "I've been knocking on John's door for two months without any response."

"Just get up there at eight and get a date."

A little before 8:00 a.m., I was standing outside John's door. We were friends, but he had been adamant that he couldn't find time for a hearing on the bill. John greeted me as he came down the hall. "Good morning, Alan. Come on in."

"John, I need to get a hearing date on the HBA."

"Sure," he said. "When do you want it?"

I couldn't believe my ears.

I was incredulous. "What the hell has happened, John?"

"Last night Mayor Daley spent the night at the White House. Lady Bird talked to him. He called me and told me to get this bill moving. If I don't do what he tells me to do, I'm dead."

Richard Daley, one of the kingpins in the national Democratic Party, controlled Chicago politics. There was no question that John's political career would end if he didn't do what Daley asked. I got a hearing date.

On the Senate side, the chairman of the highway subcommittee, Senator Jennings Randolph of West Virginia, also opposed the HBA. Jennings, too, was a friend of mine, but with strong support from the billboard industry, he likewise refused my requests for a hearing. Jennings put together a transportation budget bill that was passed out of committee to go to the Senate floor for a vote. There was no provision for the Highway Beautification bill in the legislation. The day before Jennings was to present his transportation budget legislation to the full Senate—normally a routine matter after approval by a committee—I got another call from the president.

"Alan, I want you to be up at Mike Mansfield's office tomorrow morning around nine. The transportation bill is coming up on the floor for a vote first thing. I want you to tell Mike to get Jennings to his office. Then you tell Jennings that he has to amend his bill to include funding for the HBA. After that, I want you to sit in the visitors' gallery and see that it gets done."

The idea of a committee chairman amending his own bill on the Senate floor, a bill that he had carefully tailored in committee, was not only unheard of, but anathema to his stature as a leader. It's the chairman's job to massage and tailor a bill before it *gets* to the Senate floor—a process that takes months of effort. To amend a bill on the floor is like saying, "I didn't do my job."

Senator Mike Mansfield was the majority leader of the Senate, and fortunately, another good friend of mine. I arrived at his office at 9:00 a.m. and passed along the president's request. Mike was a rather imperturbable fellow, but he had a small smile as he listened to what the president wanted. We talked for a few minutes before Mike asked his secretary to call Senator Randolph to his office.

Jennings, a portly, affable man, walked into Mike's office, slapped both of us on the back, and sat down in the chair next to mine.

"How you boys doing this morning?" he asked.

"Jennings," Mike said, "Alan has a message for you from the president."

I got right to the point. "The president asked me to come here and tell you that it's essential that you amend the highway legislation this morning," I relayed, "to include funding for the Highway Beautification Act."

Senator Randolph looked at Mike. Then he looked at me. He turned white. He turned red. He straightened his chair.

Without a word, he stood up and marched out of the office. I don't know what the president had on Jennings, but Jennings knew that he had no choice.

"That was very interesting," Mike commented wryly.

Legislation such as an authorization bill normally comes up in the morning session when there is nobody present but the president of the Senate and one or two other senators. Such legislation is normally without controversy since it has been already been approved in committee. Early mornings are too early for tourists and too routine for the press. I was the only person in the gallery.

I watched Jennings stand and address the president of the Senate. "Mr. President, without objection, I would like to amend the transportation bill."

Of course there was no objection. So the president told him to proceed.

Jennings looked directly at me. It is the only time in my life I've seen pure hatred in another's eyes. After that, Jennings never spoke to me again.

President Johnson signed the Highway Beautification Act into law in October 1965. As he did so, he said, "This bill will enrich our spirits and restore a small measure of our national greatness. Beauty belongs to all the people. And so long as I am president,

what has been divinely given to nature will not be taken reck-
lessly away by man."

The escalating number of fatalities on American highways in the
1960s was a growing concern in the country. In 1965 there were
47,087 vehicular deaths, or 5.39 fatalities per 100 million miles
traveled. In the 1966 State of the Union address, the president
proposed the Highway Safety Act.

In spite of heavy opposition by the US automakers, both
the Highway Safety Act and the National Traffic Motor Vehicle
Safety Act were signed into law in September 1966. This created
the National Highway Safety Bureau (NHSB), which was placed
in the Department of Commerce under my supervision as under
secretary for transportation. We obtained a hard-nosed, very
bright, knowledgeable doctor from New York, Bill Haddon, to
head this agency. Bill did not have a great sense of humor, and he
was not a man interested in compromise. He knew what needed
to be done and proceeded to do it.

Bill's first campaign was for mandatory seat belts. The American automobile manufacturers threw their considerable political
clout against the proposal, claiming seat belts offered no safety
benefits and that the public would rebel at the idea of spending
three hundred dollars more per vehicle for seat belts.

Henry Ford II called the White House to get the White
House to call my office to make an appointment for him to see
me. I assume this was to impress me with his influence. He could
easily have made an appointment directly with my secretary. Mr.
Ford entered my office and directly sat down.

Without preamble he began. "I'm here to say that you can forget about that damn seat-belt rule, Boyd. It's not going anywhere.

Nobody wants it, and you're wasting your time. Besides, seat belts don't do a bit of good."

It struck me that he thought he was talking to somebody who worked for him—which may have been how he felt the government should function. I told him I appreciated his thoughts.

I received similar messages from the other American car manufacturers who seemed to believe they could dictate the terms of any "safety" regulations. Their suggestions did not include driver safety. In contrast, Mr. Honda, the founder of the Honda Corporation, came to my office, saying, "I only want to be sure we understand what exactly you want us to do and we will do it."

Bill Haddon did such a powerful job of presenting safety statistics during his congressional testimony, however, that Congress was convinced. I believe that for years the automakers did everything in their power to make seat belts uncomfortable and inconvenient in the hopes that the public would hate them.

Congress, however, had made the writing of safety regulations the prerogative of the NHSB. Bill and his staff wrote the rule. After my final review, it was published and became law on March 1, 1967.

Other vehicle safety regulations followed, including requiring headrests, shatter-resistant windshields, impact-absorbing steering wheels, reinforced passenger cabins, and airbags, to name but a few. We also instituted highway safety regulations that added safer guardrails, improved street lighting, and standardized road signage.

In the media today, I hear the idea that the government is the problem, not the solution. Just with regard to automobile safety, the federal government has saved hundreds of thousands of lives by mandating vehicle and roadway improvements. Between 1966 and 2013, fatalities per 100 million vehicle miles decreased by almost 85 percent, from 7.31 to 1.09 per 100 million miles traveled.

My duties kept expanding. While I was busy with motor vehicle safety, highway beautification, maritime subsidies, and complaints from various cities about the problems created by the interstate highway routes, the president decided it was time to create a Department of Transportation (DOT).

In 1965, transportation represented about 20 percent of personal consumption expenditures. There were thirty-five agencies with transportation-related responsibilities, with a cumulative annual budget of more than $5 billion. Many of us in government had talked for years about how to improve the situation.

In 1966, President Johnson revived the idea in his State of the Union address: "I recommend that you help me modernize and streamline the federal government by creating a new cabinet-level Department of Transportation, [which] is needed to bring together our transportation activities. The present structure . . . makes it almost impossible to serve either the growing demands of this great nation or the needs of the industry, or the right of the taxpayer to full efficiency and real frugality."

Six months before the address, the president had set up a task force composed of representatives from the different transportation entities of the federal government. Charlie Zwick, the deputy director of the Bureau of the Budget, and I were co-chairmen. For some reason the name of our group was the Boyd Task Force. Our charge was to draft the organic law to present to Congress with the hope that it would be used as the basis to create the legislation for a new Department of Transportation. There were seven or eight members in all on the task force, each an expert on various aspects of the issue. Our White House liaison was Bill Moyers.

I specifically requested Cecil Mackey from the Federal Aviation Agency at the urging of the former administrator, Jeeb Halaby. I liked and respected Jeeb, and we worked well together at the CAB and the FAA to coordinate government policies and expenditures in the aviation industry. He told me, "If you ever do anything about a Department of Transportation, make sure you include Cecil." The advice was excellent. Cecil effectively ran the task force. The Department of Transportation benefited significantly because of his knowledge and skill.

The task force started with the concept that, taken as a whole, transportation constituted one system. It is not a means to an end in itself, but rather, a service that moves goods and people to help businesses and individuals achieve their goals. Given that, our first focus was to determine what needed to be included—and excluded—in the proposed Department of Transportation.

We decided the department should include functions related to transportation policy, funding, safety, and research, but exclude economic regulation. We examined thirty-five agencies to determine whether they should be included wholly or in part, or to exclude them entirely. There were large agencies we thought should be included, such as the Coast Guard and the FAA, as well as smaller agencies such as the Great Lakes Pilotage Association and the St. Lawrence Seaway Administration. We also included the Maritime Administration, the Panama Canal, the Alaskan Railroad, and the Bureau of Public Roads—which didn't have a large number of personnel, but did have an enormous budget.

Though we decided that the economic regulatory functions of the Civil Aeronautics Board and the Interstate Commerce Commission should remain independent, we determined that their transportation accident and safety investigation functions should be part of the department. However, we soon realized that to avoid any conflict of interest, safety investigation needed to be independent. We suggested the creation of a National Transportation Safety Board.

Many decisions about what to include in the department were fairly straightforward. One thorny issue, however, was what to do with urban mass transit. There were valid arguments for either placing it in the Department of Transportation or letting it remain in the Department of Housing and Urban Development. Our task force, along with the White House and the Bureau of the Budget, engaged in the debate.

The ultimate, Solomon-like decision was to leave it with Housing and Urban Development temporarily, until it could move to a new Urban Mass Transit Administration (UMTA) to be created within the DOT. Though I thought this was the right decision at the time, I now think it was a mistake. Although UMTA was "transportation," I believe HUD could have used mass transit funding to enhance and support their other development programs.

Fortunately, I don't think we made many mistakes. In fact, I think the task force did a superb job of designing an efficient government department led by a secretary, an under secretary, a deputy secretary with responsibilities like a chief operating officer, and a general counsel in charge of legal affairs. The organizational chart was structured by department-wide specialties, such as administration or policy.

We wanted to avoid organizing by transportation sectors like highways, railroad, and waterways, because we believed that could become a breeding ground for "stovepipes," a term for territorial pettiness characterized by an inability to identify with the whole organization and an unwillingness to share information. We proposed five divisions: Administration, Policy, Research and Development, International Aviation, and Public Information, each with its own assistant secretary. In addition, we suggested that the administrator of each agency in the department report directly to the secretary.

Designing a new department was time consuming. One night, Bill Moyers and I were at my office working on the legislation into the early morning. When I finally went home, Bill went back to the White House. As soon as I got home, the phone rang.

"Alan, why are you home at this hour?" said President Johnson. "You ought to be working!"

I demurred, saying that I'd just gotten home—which I figured he already knew from talking to Bill.

"Well, okay. Get some sleep," he offered, "so you can be back to work early in the morning."

That was Johnson's backhanded way of letting me know that he appreciated the amount of work I was putting in. He had a habit of doing things like that—which I found rather refreshing.

Once the task force finished the draft legislation and the White House added its stamp of approval, it was time to shop the proposed legislation around Congress.

I met with Senator John McClellan, the chairman of the Committee on Government Operations. He was fine with everything until he came to the earmarks proposal. An earmark is a provision within a bill that directs a specified amount of money to a particular project. Often this funding is for a project to benefit a congressional representative's home district.

Even back in the 1960s, the validity of earmarks, sometimes called "pork," was challenged. Our draft legislation was written to remove transportation projects from the general appropriations process and eliminate the use of earmarks. We wanted the department to perform a cost analysis on every project and report the findings to Congress, which would then vote on funding. This procedure would reduce the opportunities for pork.

After reviewing the earmarks proposal, Senator McClellan looked at me. In his wonderful Arkansas drawl he said, "Alan, that dog won't hunt." I knew right then the provision was dead. Legislation lives or dies by committee. If the chairman of the committee wants a provision out, it's out.

Another senator on that committee, Henry "Scoop" Jackson, was very concerned about protecting the environment. I believe that Scoop was the force behind a requirement added to the legislation that no highways could be built through public parks, wildlife or waterfowl refuges, or a historic site unless there was no feasible alternative. That determination was to be made solely by the secretary of the DOT. Senator Jackson deserves much credit and many thanks for his forthright contributions.

During our negotiations with Congress, we had to make a few other changes to the draft legislation as well. The shipowners and the seaman unions never forgot that I'd tried to end their subsidies. There was a possibility that I'd be named as the DOT's first secretary, since I was the senior federal official for transportation. The maritime industry used its influence at the committee level to remove the Maritime Administration from the department and therefore from any possibility of being under my control. Congress later put the Maritime Administration back in the DOT—but not until long after I was gone.

There were a few other relatively minor changes. After they were made, it was pretty smooth sailing. With bipartisan support, the legislation passed both houses of Congress. President Johnson signed it into law on October 15, 1966. At the signing, he said the following:

> We have come to this historic East Room of the White House today to establish and to bring into being a Department of Transportation, the second Cabinet office to be added to the President's Cabinet in recent months. This Department that we

are establishing will have a mammoth task—to untangle, to coordinate, and to build the national transportation system for America that America is deserving of.

And because the job is great, I intend to appoint a strong man to fill it. The new Secretary will be my principal adviser and my strong right arm on all transportation matters. I hope he will be the best-equipped man in this country to give leadership to the country, to the President, to the Cabinet, to the Congress.

The obvious question was, who was best equipped to be the first secretary?

XIV

An Honor to Serve

The consensus was that I would be the one nominated. Then a friend who was a White House assistant to the president called me to say confidentially that the president was thinking of appointing someone else to be secretary of transportation. My friend wanted me to be forewarned.

I confess that tension had been mounting within me on hearing nothing from the president. Upon receiving word from my friend in the White House, I decided to act. I called the president and told him that he didn't owe me anything and that I had been honored to serve him in the capacities to which he had appointed me. I added that if I could be of any service to him in the future, I would be happy to do so, but that I would also be happy to leave the government satisfied that I had done the best job I knew how.

"What the hell are you talking about?" the president demanded.

I told him I had heard from a confidential source that he was considering naming someone else secretary.

The president insisted that I disclose the name of the person to whom I had talked. I told him I could not.

"Are you telling your president you won't tell him who talked?"

I replied that I had given my word. I wouldn't tell him, and there was no point in discussing it further.

After a moment of silence on the line, Johnson spoke. "Alan, don't you do any damn fool thing. Just sit tight and shut up!"

A few weeks later, Flavil and I were invited down to the ranch with the president and Mrs. Johnson. This was the second time I had been invited to the ranch, but it was Flavil's first.

We flew down to Texas with John Gardner and his wife, Aida, on a Special Air Mission plane. John was an impressive guy. He had been president of the Carnegie Foundation and a professor at Stanford, and was currently the secretary of health, education, and welfare. Later, upon leaving the Johnson administration, he founded Common Cause, a grassroots organization working for public good. John told me that he had a practice of sitting in his office on Wednesday afternoons with the door closed and the phone off, making time to reflect creatively on things beyond the urgent problems of the moment. I was not alone in my enthusiasm to persuade him to run for president. He wouldn't hear of it. I think John was a truly great man, and it was an honor to be his friend.

The president and Lady Bird were at the ranch when we arrived Saturday evening. The six of us had a pleasant dinner talking about a variety of events, none of which affected me. In the morning we gathered for breakfast, then returned to our rooms to prepare for church. The president always attended church on Sundays when he was at the ranch.

Flavil and I were in our room upstairs when I heard Johnson yelling, "Alan! Alan! Where's Alan? Alan, come here!"

I went downstairs. The president asked me to come into the library. He closed the door. Without preamble he declared, "I want you to be my secretary of transportation."

"Mr. President, this is the greatest honor I've ever had, and I certainly want to do it," I replied. "I have one condition: if I am the secretary of transportation, you will make no transportation decisions without me being involved."

I knew White House assistants who were not above trying to slip things around cabinet officials to achieve their own agendas. I didn't want that to happen to me.

He agreed. We shook hands. And he was, as ever, true to his word.

Shortly after our conversation, we walked out to the driveway, where there were two automobiles waiting for our drive to church. Lady Bird was by the front car, talking to John about which car to ride in. She said, "Mr. Secretary, come join me in this car."

President Johnson said, "Which secretary are you talking about?"

With that, everyone turned and congratulated me. The president kissed Flavil on the cheek. Luci, the Johnsons' daughter, who had been upstairs with Flavil while Flavil was trying to decide whether to wear a coat because of the cool weather, turned to her and said, "Well, I guess you won't be cold any longer today!"

The president officially nominated me on November 6, 1966. Senator Warren Magnuson, chairman of the Senate Interstate and Foreign Commerce Committee, held my Senate confirmation hearing on January 11, 1967. I looked forward to the session. Maggie and I were good friends.

I was escorted into the hearing room by the two senators from Florida, my friends George Smathers and Spessard Holland. They were proud to stand with me. I was the first Floridian to serve in the cabinet. Well known in Congress by then, I was confirmed without opposition. At the White House on January 16, I was sworn in as the first secretary of the Department of Transportation.

The department was to begin operation on April 1, 1967, which gave us just a few months to organize a department with nearly 95,000 employees. It was a busy time, hiring staff, locating office space, and finding excellent people to fill the newly created executive positions.

There would be five new assistant secretaries, eight new administrators, an under secretary, a deputy secretary, and a general counsel. All of these positions were "presidential appointments." Technically, the president made these appointments and could do so without consulting me. In fact, however, I made or was consulted on every appointment but two. One, Everett Hutchinson, a lawyer from Texas who'd been chairman of the Interstate Commerce Commission, someone I knew well, was appointed as under secretary. The other, John Robson, a Republican whom I had never met, was appointed general counsel. He turned out to be a superb lawyer, a good manager, and a dear friend.

I liked Everett, but discovered he was ineffectual. I eventually went to the president and told him to give Everett a medal or something, but get him out of the department. The president did, and immediately appointed John Robson as the new under secretary—with my wholehearted approval.

I can honestly say that the department was staffed with the best people we could find without regard to political favors or party. We put together an excellent staff. My approach with these new appointees was simple: "I asked you to take this leadership position because you're an expert in your field," I told them. "If you need help, let me know. If you make progress, let me know. I don't want to know everything, but I do want to understand what's going on. Most importantly, I expect everyone to work as a team and to deal with every problem as a common problem. I will not tolerate any stovepipes."

I was particularly aware that in creating a new organization comprising preexisting, independent agencies, there is always a danger of groups keeping information to themselves. The new department required a mind-set of cooperation, not separation.

The group of leaders I selected worked together wonderfully as a unified team. They made the new Department of Transportation an outstanding organization. Each made unique contributions, but there were a few standouts in my mind.

Alan Dean was my chief administration officer and the consummate bureaucrat, a term I use with great admiration in his case. He was a career public servant who knew everything there was to know about how our government functioned. He was honest, hard-nosed, and competent.

Cecil Mackey was my assistant secretary for policy. He'd been my right-hand man on the DOT task force. Cecil was bright, accomplished, and an idealist. He was also distinctive in that, unlike most people, he had no problem telling me when he thought I was wrong. There isn't anyone from those years whom I thought of as a better friend.

Jo Philipovic was my wonderful, loyal secretary. I could not have survived without her. Jo had been my secretary at the CAB. I would have taken her with me to the Commerce Department, assuming she'd agreed, but that position had come with a secretary. Jo understood my foibles and I understood hers—though I can't remember her having any.

Dick Copaken was my White House fellow. He basically showed up on my doorstep saying that he'd been assigned as my full-time aide for a year. My response was, "You're just the man I need!" I immediately put him in charge of creating a grand opening celebration on April 1. I told him, "I want to have a big show, and I want you to set it up." That was nearly the only direction he got from me.

Also on my superb team were Paul Sitton, deputy secretary; Admiral Willard Smith, commandant of the Coast Guard; James Irwin, Coast Guard attaché; General Bozo McKee, Federal Aviation administrator; Don Agger, assistant secretary for international aviation; Joe McCann, St. Lawrence Seaway administrator; John Sweeney, assistant secretary for public information; Frank Lehan, assistant secretary for research; Langhorne Bond, my special assistant; and John Kennedy, my office executive secretary. These people worked together to create one of the most productive and happy periods of my life.

As part of the department, we created two new agencies, the Federal Highway Administration and the Federal Railroad Administration. Lowell Bridwell was appointed as the first Federal Highway administrator. He knew highways, and he knew what needed to be done and took care to do it. He wasted no time. He did an excellent job organizing that agency

Scheffer Lang became the first Federal Railroad administrator. Shef was new to government, but he knew and loved trains, and was dedicated to his work. He ingratiated himself to me when, during his maiden speech as administrator, he told the Association of American Railroads that one of the railroads' major problems was the inadequacy of railroad management. I thought he was right. Shef was a Republican, which I liked. I wanted the department to be completely nonpartisan. Transportation is ultimately not about politics—but service.

The months leading up to our April start were consumed in large part with filling the many positions and introducing myself to the various agencies. I always asked how I could be helpful, gave people my contact information, and invited them to call if they had any ideas.

I also spent a significant amount of time communicating with Congress, particularly the Interstate and Foreign Commerce Committee, and the Appropriations Committee in both houses. I knew exploring their ideas for the department would be productive.

The Washington headquarters for the department would need office space for about five hundred people. With the new DOT building still under construction, we had offices all over town. We used three floors of the Federal Aviation Building, which housed my office.

We also had offices in a building at Sixth and D Streets, in the ICC Building, the Matomic Building, and the Universal Building, as well as a few other buildings on Indiana Avenue. I joked at my Senate confirmation hearing that we'd probably pitch tents on the Mall to take care of all other staff.

Setting up my office was a priority. I had two requirements: a conference room and a bedroom. I knew there would be times, most likely during emergencies, when I needed to remain at the office around the clock.

Soon after I'd moved in, I got a call from Jack Anderson, considered by some to be the father of investigative journalism. His muckraking column, the Washington Merry-Go-Round, which he wrote with Drew Pearson, was syndicated in more than 650 newspapers.

"I just want to let you know, Boyd, that we're printing a column tomorrow about how you've spent over two hundred and fifty thousand dollars on your new office," he announced.

With everything I had to do, I needed this like I needed a hole in the head.

"Whoever gave you that information doesn't know what they're talking about. Why don't you send someone over to see my office before you print that column?"

"It's not fancy?" he asked me.

"Come take a look."

A journalist came to my office the next day. I showed him my modest office, my government-issue desk, and the adjoining cramped room with a small cot. It took little convincing that there was nothing grandiose about it. The column never ran.

As a team-building activity, we had a contest to design a logo for the department and invited all DOT employees to participate. Our volunteer judges were from the Metropolitan Museum of Art, the National Museum, and the Heraldry section of the Department of Defense. The contest was a big hit. Submissions poured in. I was pleased with the winning design, a modified triskelion, which looks something like three bent human legs set in a triangular pattern. The legs represented transportation on land, sea, and air.

The department opened for business on April 1, 1967. I was impressed that all of the staff in their many locations came to work that day to find a directory on their desk with phone numbers for everyone in all DOT agencies. Alan Dean, my chief administration officer, was responsible for that. Organizational efficiency and responsiveness were important to me. I set in place a process where every incoming letter or call to my office received a response within forty-eight hours.

The opening-day celebration that Dick Copaken organized was impressive. I was driven from the DOT office to the Mall in a horse-drawn carriage. There were public events in the Natural

History Museum and the American History Museum. Several blocks of the Mall were covered with activities: a balloon ride, a hovercraft, and a man flying with a jetpack. Transportation, its history and its future, were on display. It was a wonderful day, and well attended by the public.

The unification of several dozen different agencies was not without its problems. The FAA had been an independent agency. Being forced to join the department caused it a lot of heartburn, because it had the classic stovepipe mentality. It also suffered from NIH disease—Not Invented Here syndrome. No matter what you wanted it to do or what change you suggested, its response was classically, "That's not the way we do it here." Their people believed they were smarter than everyone else. As a consequence, both while I was with the DOT and later, the United States lagged behind other developed countries in air traffic technology.

Whereas the FAA felt like it'd been put in prison, the Coast Guard, transferred from the Treasury Department, felt like it'd been paroled. The Coast Guard was made up of people whom I came to admire without reservation. They were very frugal, modest, hardworking, and intelligent. They valued being totally cooperative, and would seek out opportunities to be helpful in other areas of the department. It was the greatest organization I have ever worked with, and it had a profound, positive influence on the culture of the department.

After my Senate confirmation as secretary of transportation, I began to attend cabinet meetings. This was not a new experience for me. I had attended several cabinet meetings while I was at the Commerce Department when Secretary Connor was out of town. The cabinet room was rectangular. The large rectangular table in the middle of the room was surrounded by large black leather armchairs. A brass plaque on the back of each chair indicated the office of the secretary who was to sit in that chair.

The chairs were placed in order of the date the department was created. Mine was farthest from the president.

In addition to cabinet meetings, I went to the White House about every three weeks when the president invited me to lunch in his private quarters. During these lunches, alone with him, LBJ was the best—and most attentive—listener I have ever encountered. He would fix his eyes on me and ask what was going on with transportation. What kinds of problems was I having? What had I done? Johnson also had the uncanny ability to retain everything I told him. Once he quoted a conversation—word for word—that we'd had five years earlier.

These lunches were nearly all business. He was a hands-on president who did not like to be surprised. He met with his cabinet secretaries routinely. His retention of detail was impressive, but Johnson was also an incredibly hard worker. It was said that he got up at 6:00 a.m. every morning, worked until midafternoon, then took a brief nap. Then he was up again and worked until about 2:00 a.m. That gave the president essentially two full workdays—every day.

Cabinet meetings were normally held in the morning every second Tuesday, and lasted an hour and a half. The cabinet room was adjacent to the Oval Office. The president would take three steps from the Oval Office to his seat in the cabinet room to preside over the meetings. There was no small talk. The cabinet members said their hellos before he arrived, and after he sat down, all conversation focused on the agenda the president had prepared. He informed each secretary if he wanted a report from them. He was formal, addressing each of us by title, asking us pointedly to report on the specific issue that he was interested in.

Sometimes the president might solicit support for a cause. "Secretary Weaver is having trouble with the Fair Housing Act," he might say. "I want you fellows to go up on the Hill and help him get that legislation passed. Can I count on you?"

Every cabinet member would nod and say, "Yes, sir!" But I don't think any of us ever complied. It wasn't disobedience, but a shared understanding that each of us worked hard to build goodwill with members of Congress—which we were dependent on to advance our own causes.

The issues I had to report on were nowhere as complex as Vietnam—the biggest issue on the president's plate. Highway safety was an ongoing struggle as seat-belt regulations took effect. The automakers resisted improvements at every turn, hoping to dissuade the public from their use. Dealing with the railroads presented some challenges, too, since railroad management had a philosophical objection to government intervention. They opposed the eight-mile test track the department was building near Pueblo, Colorado. We planned on testing such things as wheels and car connectors to improve rail safety and efficiency. In spite of their resistance to government involvement, however, they were quite willing to accept subsidies for new equipment and upgrades to their infrastructure.

The most controversial issue for aviation was the Supersonic Speed Transport, or SST. The government had been involved in a debate about an SST since the Kennedy administration. A passenger plane designed to fly faster than the speed of sound would cut the travel time from New York to London in half. The first SST project, the Concorde, was a joint French and British effort. A short time after the Concorde was announced, the Russian government declared its intention to develop a supersonic plane, the Tu-144. At the time, Jeeb Halaby, the FAA administrator, told

President Kennedy that the American aerospace industry could lose 50,000 jobs and $4 billion if it didn't develop an American SST.

The FAA asked the American aerospace manufacturers to submit proposals to design an SST. Boeing was the eventual winner. It spawned an unusual arrangement, the government paying a private company to design a civilian plane.

Though the SST seemed like the future of passenger air travel, it was costly, inefficient—consuming six times more fuel than a 747—and twice as loud as a 747 on takeoff and landing. Worse was the sonic boom associated with breaking the sound barrier. This thunderous boom spreads out behind a plane like the wake of a ship.

My involvement with the SST began in 1964 when I was appointed to the president's advisory committee on the SST. Committee members included the secretaries of commerce and treasury, the director of the CIA, and the administrators of both the National Aeronautics and Space Administration and the FAA. Charles Lindbergh was also on the committee. Our chairman, Bob McNamara, secretary of defense, was a strong opponent of the SST.

I favored a supersonic passenger plane, as I believed US manufacturers needed it to stay competitive in the global market. Historically, humans have been enamored with speed and have always been willing to pay a premium for it. I assumed that would be true with the SST.

The FAA conducted a study to measure the public's reaction to a steady diet of sonic booms. Oklahoma City was the guinea pig. It was chosen because it was flat, had a variety of buildings, and had experienced sonic booms from military planes in the past. For almost six months the city was treated to an average of eight sonic booms a day.

The reaction was definitely unfavorable. More than 15,000 complaints and 4,900 claims were filed for cracked glass, broken plaster, cracked chimneys, and loosened roof tiles. The testing was stopped. It was clear that the only possible routes for an SST were across oceans. It was decided that there would be no SST flights over the United States, and in 1971, despite support from President Nixon, the Senate ended funding for the project.

I should note that the French and the British did build the Concorde. It commenced transatlantic passenger service in 1976 between New York and Paris and London. Later in my career, as chairman of Airbus Industrie of North America, I often flew to France on the Concorde and could cross the Atlantic in three and a half hours, just half the usual flight time. At supersonic speed, coupled with the six-hour time difference between France and the United States, technically I would arrive in the United States before I "left" Paris. Unfortunately, Concorde flights were discontinued in 2003.

The elephant that was always in the room during cabinet meetings was the Vietnam War. For all the good Johnson did domestically, his escalation of the number of American troops in Vietnam, from about 20,000 to 535,000, was highly unpopular with the public. From his first days as president, he was losing support in Congress. Cabinet meetings almost always started with Secretary of Defense Bob McNamara, or Dick Helms, head of the CIA, giving the daily body count. It didn't take many such reports in my early days as a cabinet member to grow suspicious. The ratio was always roughly ten Viet Cong killed for each American. It seemed curious to me, therefore, how there could be no progress in the war when we seemed to be killing so many Vietnamese.

Once, when Vice President Hubert Humphrey returned from a two-week trip to Southeast Asia, the president asked him to provide an update. Hubert took off in his rapid-fire way of speaking. He was like an open faucet, speaking in a constant, uninterrupted stream of words. He never took a breath.

As Hubert droned, the president began to list to one side, his head resting in his hand. He reached under the table and buzzed for his orderly, who brought him a root beer. The president finished his drink before Hubert completed his more than half-hour verbal display. Without a question or saying thank you, the president called on the next person.

There was no discussion unless the president asked for comments. And Vietnam, we all knew, was not open for discussion—even if the president asked for it. Once, out of frustration, the president blurted, "Tell me what to do about Vietnam! Just tell me what to do!"

Everyone—or nearly everyone—in the room knew that he really didn't want anyone telling him anything. He just didn't know what to do about the war. After the meeting, one cabinet member, Bill Wertz, I believe, who was secretary of labor, followed the president into the Oval Office.

"Mr. President, you've just got to get us out of Vietnam," Wertz supposedly told President Johnson. To my knowledge, the president never spoke to him again.

It became increasingly clear that the Vietnam War was taking a heavy toll on the nation. Secretary of Defense McNamara came to the conclusion that the United States could not win the war. In early November 1967 he sent a memorandum to President Johnson recommending that the United States stop bombing North Vietnam and turn the ground fighting over to the South Vietnamese. McNamara was basically admitting that the US military strategy had failed.

I don't know firsthand, but I read that Bob never heard back from the president on his recommendations. On November 29, McNamara resigned to become president of the World Bank.

There was a reception for Bob on the tenth floor of the State Department, in a beautiful room decorated with historical items, including furniture from Thomas Jefferson. It was a large gathering. All of the cabinet secretaries and their wives were present. Partway through the reception, Flavil noticed Bob standing off by himself, looking like the loneliest man in the world.

"We should go talk to him," she said to me.

Bob was cordial, yet I couldn't help but see how miserable he was. I think the pressure of failure weighed on him. We could not change that, but Flavil didn't want him to have to stand alone at his own reception.

I noted with pride how Flavil had blossomed in Washington, from our early experience at the Blair House reception to her compassionate awareness in this sensitive moment. Even at White House functions, Flavil impressed the assembled reporters. At one state dinner, she entered wearing a beautiful green dress she had designed and sewn herself. Reporters clambered to know the name of the designer of her gown. She smiled as she replied, "It's an original Flavil." Flavil was ever original.

The next presidential election year approached, and New Hampshire held the first Democratic primary in March. Anti-war candidate Eugene McCarthy came within seven points of beating the president. Johnson's public approval rating was a dismal 36 percent.

Believing that even if he could be reelected, his candidacy would divide the country, he decided to not seek reelection. Hubert Humphrey became the Democratic nominee that August. Just weeks before Election Day, Flavil and I were again invited to the LBJ ranch.

It was a beautiful, warm October weekend. Late one evening the president invited everyone to go for a swim. Flavil and I were the only ones to accept. We were in the pool when Johnson started talking about how ticked off he was at Hubert because he was campaigning as an anti–Vietnam War candidate. His anger shifted to mimicry. He got Flavil and me laughing with his pitch-perfect imitation of Hubert's mannerisms, voice, and rat-a-tat-tat way of speaking. Johnson was forever studying people, and he was a good mimic. He remembered not only what people said, but also how they said it.

I thought Johnson was an excellent president, though the war cast a dark shadow over his presidency. I think it damaged his heart in every sense of the word. He left office in January 1969 and died of a heart attack in 1972. I hope these many years later, the public and historians have come to appreciate all the good that LBJ achieved domestically—as well as gained an appreciation for the deep and genuine concern he had for the people of America.

The president once told me a story about when he taught Mexican Americans in school in southwest Texas. He hadn't grown up with much, but he'd never realized just how poor people could be until that experience. He hated seeing those bright kids growing up deprived of the opportunity to succeed. He told me, "We ought to do better in this country." I never saw President Johnson be anything but sincere when it came to the public good. He was a great man and a great American.

When Richard Nixon was elected in November 1968, I had to decide whether to look for another position in Washington or leave. I considered running for the Senate in Florida. My good friend and longtime supporter Senator Holland told me he wasn't going to run for reelection in 1970, and Spessard said he would like to see me elected as his successor.

I was flattered—and interested. I weighed the pros and cons. Working in the government, I had done many interesting things and met a lot of wonderful people. I believed it was noble work and that I had helped to better my country. I enjoyed being part of the White House and Washington inner circles, with perks like flying on Air Force One and attending state dinners.

In spite of the positives, working in Washington was trying and demanding. I served in three organizations—the CAB, the Department of Commerce, and the Department of Transportation. Each position was more time consuming than the one before. After ten years I was tired. Flavil and I decided we would move back to Miami and resume a quieter life. I knew I could practice law with Hardy and Dick.

In retrospect, I believe that had I been elected to the Senate, which was highly possible with Senator Holland's support, I would have been a one- or at most two-term senator. As a liberal Democrat, I might have survived the Carter years, but I never would have survived the Reagan years.

Not long after Humphrey lost to Nixon, Bill Johnson came to see me. Bill was president of IC Industries, which owned the Illinois Central Railroad. Bill was looking for someone to run the railroad portion of the business. He said he was too busy diversifying IC Industries into everything from manufacturing to Midas Mufflers to be able to focus on running a railroad. He asked me to be president of the Illinois Central Railroad.

The position appealed to me immensely. I'd seen plenty of poorly managed railroads, going back to my time with the Florida Railroad and Public Utilities Commission. I'd always thought that I could do a better job. Living in Chicago also appealed to me. I told Bill I'd take the job. We discussed a few details. As he was leaving, Bill dropped a bomb.

"Oh, by the way," he said, almost as an afterthought, "you should probably know that we've got an application before the DOT for money to replace our commuter fleet."

If that wasn't a conflict of interest, I don't know what was. I immediately picked up the phone and called John Robson, who was now my under secretary. I told John about the job offer and that I hadn't known anything about the application. In the normal course of business, the secretary of the department wouldn't follow specific issues like the IC's application unless a problem developed.

"For God's sake, John, don't let anything about that application come into my office," I told him. "I don't want to know one thing about it—how much is involved, whether it's going to be approved, not approved, anything! Period!"

I left my position as secretary of transportation on January 20, 1969. Flavil and I had decided that a trip around the world would be a good way to decompress from our active life in Washington. A few days later, she and I left for a nine-week world tour. I boarded the plane in Washington with a copy of the *Chicago Daily News* to start my transition to life in Chicago. Flying over the Rockies I read an article—an "exposé"—about my becoming president of the IC after the IC was awarded millions by the DOT. The article clearly implied that I had bought myself a nice job with taxpayers' money. I was deeply upset, not the least because no reporter had made an attempt to contact me or check the facts on the subject.

I realized this might set off an investigation with committee hearings, requiring testimony, possibly from me. I needed to get in touch with someone before we left the country. Fortunately we had a layover in California. I found a pay phone and called

Congressman Bob Poage of Texas. We knew each other, though not well.

I said, "I want to tell you that I've done nothing inappropriate. If you want to talk to someone who knows, talk to Under Secretary John Robson. He's a Republican with no political interest in covering my tracks. He will tell you exactly what happened."

The congressman was gracious. He said they would get in touch with me if need be, and told me to go ahead with my trip.

Flavil and I spent four days in Tahiti and saw sights that would have been fit for paintings by Gauguin. On arriving at the airport for our flight to New Zealand, we discovered that I must have erred in the schedule. There were no seats for us on the plane, and there wasn't another flight for five days. Stranded in Tahiti, we went by motor launch to the nearby island of Moorea, where we found an idyllic hotel. Our "room" was a hut on stilts above the bay. We had a bedroom, bathroom, and small porch. Water lapped below, and a breeze cooled the porch where we relaxed. By the time we caught the next plane to Auckland, I was glad I had made that mistake.

In New Zealand we were awed by the beauty of the glaciers and enjoyed the friendliness of the people. We then flew to Australia, where we were met at the Sydney airport by Don Anderson, the Australian director general of civil aviation. Don was a big, burly, former football and cricket player who radiated friendliness and fun. He and I had first met during negotiations in India in 1960. Our friendship had grown over the years during his visits to the United States.

As he and his wife gave us a warm greeting, I noticed several uniformed men waiting nearby. I asked Don who they were.

"They're your crew!" he replied.

Don had arranged for an airplane and crew to take us wherever we wished while we were in Australia. We took full advantage of that wonderful hospitality and visited Adelaide, Melbourne, Canberra, and Alice Springs. In Alice Springs, Don's friend Eddie Connellan invited us to stay on his small cattle station. Small by Australian standards, it covered almost 1,200 square miles, a spread roughly the size of Rhode Island.

Leaving Australia, we went on to visit Indonesia, Bali, Singapore, Malaysia, Hong Kong, Thailand, and Burma before finally arriving in India. In New Delhi, we were invited to stay in the American Embassy. We were guests there along with an American ambassador and his wife who themselves were on tour, traversing the world in the opposite direction to our tour.

During my visit to India in 1960, I had written Flavil in my most passionate prose about seeing the Taj Mahal in the moonlight. I had no expectation that an inanimate object could move me so profoundly. The Taj, in that light, was unlike anything I had ever experienced. It was of absolute manifest beauty and perfection. Overwhelmed with emotion, I couldn't decide if I was laughing or crying. I told Flavil of my desire to one day stand in front of the Taj, under the light of the moon, and share that magic with her. Nine years later, it seemed the time had finally come.

We set our plans to see the Taj Mahal that night. Unfortunately, our host, the ambassador, insisted that I join him and the "other ambassador" staying at the compound for a tour of the local green revolution program. This was a Rockefeller Foundation effort to help farmers increase crop yields through improved seeds and agricultural management. As his guest, I felt compelled to comply. The two-day tour consumed our available time in India. As a result, my desire to share the Taj Mahal in the moonlight with Flavil was never realized. It was a great disappointment for both of us, one I still regret.

The rest of the trip was as wonderful as the start. Iran, Greece, Italy, Spain, and Portugal were delightful, packed with art, architecture, and culture. In Greece we went to Delphi on Mount Parnassus. Failing to find the Oracle, we settled on a meal in a nearby country inn. It was one of the best meals I've eaten in my life.

Both exhausted and refreshed, we arrived in Chicago on March 30 to find that the House Ethics Committee investigation of the grants received by the railroad had found nothing wrong. On April 1, 1969, I became president of the Illinois Central Railroad.

XV

The Illinois Central

Our transition to living in Chicago was exciting. The air in Chicago seemed filled with vitality that infused our prospects for the future. Flavil and I bought a spacious apartment in a stately brick building with a stunning view of Lake Michigan at 999 North Lake Shore Drive. Earlier, while I had lived in Washington, I had become friends with Paul Nitze, the deputy secretary of defense, whose sister, Elizabeth "Pussy" Paepcke, lived in Chicago. Coincidentally, Pussy lived in the same building, a delightful bonus. She and her husband, industrialist Walter Paepcke, founded the Aspen Institute and the Aspen Music Festival. Pussy was a "grande dame" of Chicago. She welcomed us like treasured relatives. She introduced us to people dedicated to culture, the arts, and historic preservation. The "can-do" spirit, openness, and warmth of these new friends made us delighted to call Chicago home.

Chicago was a wealthy city that gave generously to charities. The business community was expected to be supportive of these efforts. I had been in Chicago only a few months when the president of the *Chicago Tribune* called. "We think it's time for you to head the United Way campaign, Alan."

I told him I barely knew my way to the men's room, and certainly didn't know the people necessary for a successful fund-raising campaign. "We'll help you. You'll have plenty of support. You'll get it done," he said. And he was right. All I had to do was ask for it, and help was given. Everybody pitched in. It was a wonderful way to meet a group of civically active and socially involved people while getting to know the city.

My transition to the railroad was not as smooth or easy. Bill Johnson had told me the Illinois Central (IC) was in great physical and financial condition. I began learning that unfortunately, neither was true. In fact, declining revenues had resulted in decades of neglect, leaving the rolling stock, the depots, and especially the rail yards in deplorable condition. Derailments were so common that people just shrugged when they occurred, then set to work putting things back together. Fortunately, most derailments happened at low speeds in the rail yards, not on the main line. But sadly, on June 10, 1971, the overnight train from Chicago to New Orleans, the Panama Limited, derailed in Tonti, Illinois. Eleven people were killed. Many more were injured.

Financially, the Illinois Central Railroad was not in good shape either. It had the second-lowest revenue per ton-mile—one ton of freight moved one mile—in the industry. Before my arrival, the IC had agreed to merge with the Gulf, Mobile and Ohio—which had the lowest ton-mile yield. Compounding our financial challenge was the location and route structure of our tracks.

The majority of the Illinois Central tracks ran north–south, whereas the bulk of the rail freight traffic in the United States moved east–west. Additionally, the Mississippi River ran more or less parallel to our major routes, forcing us to compete against the river barge carriers.

As bad as the physical and financial condition of the railroad was, I faced a still larger impediment. Many employees, both labor and management, were third- or fourth-generation Illinois Central workers—who believed they were still operating their fathers' railroad. All too often I heard the unfortunate refrain, "But that's the way my daddy did it." On top of that, the relationship between labor and management was hampered by generations of distrust. The only thing that the two groups seemed to agree upon was a resistance to innovation and change.

Even still, I was confident that my vision and drive could transform the railroad into an efficient twentieth-century transportation company. My first objective was to get my senior staff working together. I wanted them to function as a team, to share not only each other's problems, but also one another's possibilities for success. This was a new concept. Though departments were not competitive, when problems arose, such as a derailment or accident, they were quick to blame each other. The IC had a deeply entrenched "stovepipe" culture.

I instituted weekly staff meetings at which each member of my team reported on the activities, problems, and opportunities within his department. I wanted them more concerned about the railroad as a whole—and less so about their separate, individual departments. Some thought staff meetings were a good idea. Others seemed to roll their eyes, suggesting they were a waste of time. The wide range of personality styles in the group was also a challenge. Some were taciturn and said as little as they could, and others were so opinionated about everything that I had to cut them off.

I gained some progress in managing my staff, but I slammed into a stone wall with the labor union. Labor costs were a major element of the railroad's operating budget. Such costs were often dictated by labor work rules that were either negotiated with the unions or occasionally legislated by Congress. Gerald Stuckey, general chairman of the United Transportation Union, the largest union representing IC employees, possessed a psychopathic animosity for railroad management. Interestingly, his brother was the vice president of the Gulf, Mobile and Ohio (GM&O), which merged with the IC in 1972 to form the Illinois Central Gulf Railroad (ICG). I don't know the basis for Gerald's pathological distaste for management, but he was a dedicated foe of the railroad. I had never met a man like him before.

I tried to develop cordial relations with Stuckey, to engage him in the process of turning the IC around. I invited him to my office, where we talked for hours, describing possible strategies to increase employment and going over the financial numbers of the railroad. I should say I talked, as he would sit impassively, never making a comment or asking a question—even when encouraged. When I finished, he would say thank you and leave. He was as intractable as Paul Hall, the maritime union leader I'd encountered years before—but Stuckey was minus the charm. I eventually discovered that Stuckey and the unions had the erroneous belief that management kept two sets of books, and that a hidden "accurate" set would prove the railroad was making plenty of money.

I had two young men working in my office, David Gunn and Harry Meislahn, who were Harvard business school graduates. They were both on their way to becoming two of the best railroad men in the country. At my direction, David and Harry devised a five-point plan to turn the IC around. Three of five actions required concessions by the union, significantly including a revised definition of an eight-hour workday.

In 1916, Congress defined a railroad worker's day as 150 miles for passenger trains and 100 miles for freight trains, which then took about eight hours to run. In the intervening fifty years, train speed more than doubled. In 1971, a worker could finish a "day" in two and half to three hours and earn overtime wages for the additional mileage—even though it took less than eight hours. This required the railroad to either stop a train every 100 miles and change crews, or pay excessive overtime wages. We knew the unions wouldn't give this up easily. But we planned to offer the enticement of greater job stability and increased employment.

David and Harry used graphs, charts, and display boards to clearly present the plan to top officials of the United Transportation Union in Cleveland. The president of the union, Al Chesser, was a friend of mine. I thought it was an excellent plan: employees would work eight-hour days regardless of distance; management would determine the size of crews; no current employees would be laid off; all current employees would receive full wages until retirement; and disputes between the railroad and the union would be decided by a three-person panel, one from management, one from the union, and a third selected by the two.

The result of implementing the plan would be increased profitability for the railroad and a substantial number of new jobs for the union. We offered to give the accounting firm of the union's choice access to our books to validate the numbers and verify the projected benefits. I thought the hour-and-a-half presentation was brilliant.

When it was over, my friend Al looked at me and said, "Alan, you can go to hell."

What Al Chesser, Gerald Stuckey, and others failed to grasp was how profoundly the railroad industry had changed since WWII.

Until the end of the war, most passengers and freight moved by rail. But by 1950, most people owned cars. By 1960, the Interstate Highway System was making car and truck travel more convenient and economical, and jets were making air travel more efficient.

Railroads could not compete. Between 1945 and my arrival at the IC in 1970, noncommuter rail passenger travel declined 84 percent, and the rail share of the freight market shrank from 70 to 35 percent. Twenty percent of all railroads had gone bankrupt. The IC itself had gone from seventy thousand employees to twenty thousand. I thought the railroad industry—the owners, managers, and unions—could work together to save the sinking ship. To my dismay, the exact opposite was true.

The Southern Railway offered an example of how unwilling unions were to make concessions. The Southern was one of the first to replace steam locomotives with diesel engines, eliminating the need for a fireman to shovel coal into a boiler. The Southern didn't lay off a single fireman, but slowly phased out the position through attrition and reassignment. The Brotherhood of Locomotive Firemen filed a complaint, and a federal court ordered the Southern to resume hiring firemen.

The president of the Southern, Bill Brosnan, a very hard-nosed leader, complied with the court order by hiring mostly black men who were no younger than seventy.

"All they have to do," Brosnan is reported to have said, "is climb into the locomotive, sit still, and do nothing."

This featherbedding went on for another twenty years. In 1985, a mediation board finally ruled that firemen were no longer required by law for a function that did not exist on diesel trains. That reduced the required train crew to four, although some states maintained laws requiring crews of five or even six.

My experience with the United Transport Union depressed me, something I am not susceptible to often. Dysfunctional labor rules and unnecessary labor costs were eating the railroad alive. There could be no real change without union understanding and agreement. I had to do something to turn the IC around, I just didn't know what.

A new idea that held promise was transporting shipping containers by rail. More freight was being moved in containers, a departure from the old norm of transporting it by loading it into boxcars. Trucking companies were adapting to the shipping container market by meeting the containers at the port and then conveying them to their overland destination. I thought the railroad could move containers over a long distance faster and cheaper than trucks. However, to do so, we needed to operate special trains, free of the current crippling work rules that required large crews and frequent stops for crew changes.

I approached Gerald Stuckey with the idea. I assured him that there would be no job loss, that it indeed would be new business that added jobs. I wanted the union to vote to allow two-man crews to run an express container freight train from New Orleans to Chicago. The crews would get paid the top rate for the run.

Gerald refused to even present the offer to his union members for discussion or vote.

Fortunately, not all union leaders were oppositional. The Gulf, Mobile and Ohio (GM&O) had lost a lot of jobs when it merged with the IC to form the Illinois Central Gulf Railroad (ICG). I approached the union representative for the GM&O and proposed the same idea for the old GM&O tracks between Saint Louis and Chicago. This proposal was outside Stuckey's jurisdiction.

The GM&O union leader, understanding that a two-man crew was better than no crew, agreed. The train was given top priority on the tracks so the crew could highball down the line at full speed—a railroader's dream. These runs became the most desired among crews. As soon as they were posted at the union hall, senior engineers snapped them up. Crews earned good money, and the railroad made a profit, a true win-win. When members of Stuckey's union asked why there weren't any express trains from New Orleans to Chicago, Gerald told them that the railroad management refused to let them have one, which was a lie. He simply had never taken my proposal to his union members.

I had expected a fight from the unions, but it was my fellow board members at the Association of American Railroads (AAR) who truly disappointed me. The AAR's board was made up of the presidents of the thirty-or-so Class 1 railroads in the country. We met every other month in Washington. With my experience at the CAB and in transportation regulation and law at the Florida Railroad and Public Utilities Commission, and my view of the benefit of transportation working as an overall integrated service system, I saw two things the AAR board could do improve the industry's profitability: first, break free of the unnecessary and stifling regulation of the Interstate Commerce Commission (ICC); second, negotiate with the trucking industry to regain some of the lost long-haul freight business while simultaneously maximizing the efficiency of the overall transportation system.

Trucks were clearly the most efficient mode for transporting freight five hundred miles or less. Beyond that, railroads won hands down. At the time, however, an enormous amount of freight traveled from Chicago to San Francisco, or Boston to LA, by truck. It made sense to me that the railroads should try to get part of that business back.

My fellow board members were not interested in negotiating with truckers. They dismissed my proposal as misguided. Their attitude was, "Why would we negotiate with the sons of bitches who took our business away in the first place?"

Further, the idea of breaking free from the ICC seemed to scare the railroad presidents. They responded as if I had suggested taking away their security blanket. Like people at the Illinois Central, most railroad presidents had long histories in the railroad industry. Too long. They could not imagine functioning beyond "the way we've always done it." The ICC was created in 1887 to regulate the railroad monopolies and prevent abuses. The commission was a fixture in the working life of these presidents. They perceived the ICC to be as necessary to the operation of the railroads as the tracks the trains ran on.

I approached the issue differently. I had in my career been both a regulator and a commissioner. I was friends with the ICC commissioners, having played golf and gone camping with some of them. I did not view the role of government regulation as rigid and immutable, but rather as one that should adjust to the changing demands of the transportation industry. By 1970, the ICC no longer set rates, but would approve or disapprove the rates requested and justified by the railroads. The process took twelve to eighteen months, which effectively meant that railroads lacked the flexibility to adjust their rates to reflect changing conditions. During the fall grain harvest, for example, millions of tons of grain had to be hauled to ports. Truck and barge companies increased their rates in response to the demand, but the railroads weren't able to profit by the same means.

The ICC also regulated rates because the average rail freight car was transported by an average of 2.3 different railroads to reach its destination. Consequently, railroads had to collaborate on the rates they charged. Normally "colluding between competitors" would be an anti-trust violation. Congress granted an anti-trust exemption as long as the ICC reviewed rates to prevent abuse.

A typical example was the Burlington Northern's contract with Indiana Power to haul coal from Wyoming to Indianapolis. Burlington Northern tracks went as far as Centralia, Illinois. The Illinois Central was the only option to haul the coal from Centralia to Indianapolis. Burlington Northern had to negotiate a rate with the Illinois Central, which was then factored into the request the BN submitted to the ICC for approval.

The railroad industry of 1970 was definitely not the infamous "robber baron" monopoly of the 1880s. Railroads were no longer the only transportation option for shippers. By the latter half of the twentieth century, there was significant competition from other modalities that would prevent the abuses that originally led to the creation of the ICC.

I believed railroads would be better off without the ICC. As free enterprises, they would be able to respond to market pressures by shopping for the least expensive routes wherever possible, and hiking prices during periods of high demand—like the truck and barge carriers. They also would no longer require the anti-trust exemption.

All but one of my fellow AAR board members rejected my proposals. They thought that without the ICC and the negotiated rates, doing business would be too chaotic. Since most of the railroads were suffering financially under the existing arrangement, their logic seemed to me to follow the line of, "Although we will lose money on every freight car, we plan to make it up in volume."

Jack Fishwick, president of the Norfolk and Western Railroad, was my lone ally. Jack and I did our best to promote change and competition. I wouldn't say that we were laughed at, but we were relegated to the lunatic fringe of the table. We eventually gave up trying.

As a postscript, the railroad industry was substantially deregulated later in 1980 when Congress passed the Staggers Act proposed by President Jimmy Carter the previous year. The ICC was abolished in 1995, and the industry began to rebound. Since then, ton-miles have trended upward. Rail productivity gains have been among the highest of all US industries. The average railroad return on investment increased from 4.4 percent in the 1980s to 9.2 percent in the 2000s. Deregulation and free enterprise reinvigorated the railroads. Jack Fishwick and I might have earlier been viewed as on the fringe, but we were clearly prophets before our time.

In spite of the frustrations I encountered dealing with an industry that believed it was still operating in the previous century, there was one remnant of that earlier period that I greatly enjoyed: the private railcar. The Illinois Central's president's private car had pleasant sleeping quarters for guests and a president's bedroom equipped with a king-size bed. We had a kitchen and a dining area staffed by our own cook and waiter. With the car attached to the end of the train, we would sit in the comfortable parlor and watch the tracks and countryside roll out behind us.

Flavil and I took advantage of the private car as often as we could, sometimes traveling with friends and sometimes with business associates. We would visit the fascinating cities the ICG served: Memphis, Tennessee; Mobile, Alabama; Jackson, Mississippi; and New Orleans. We could leave Chicago in the late afternoon attached to the Panama Limited and arrive in New Orleans the next morning. We brought along our folding bikes and would ride around the French Quarter, or we would drive out to see antebellum plantations. Once we took members of the Chicago City Council to Louisville for the Kentucky Derby. We were fortunate to experience rail travel as it had been at the height of its elegance.

As president of the IC, I was elected to both the board of the Illinois Central Railroad and the board of Illinois Central Industries (ICI). IC Industries was a holding company created by selling IC railroad property and using the proceeds to establish a corporation to diversify into other business sectors. ICI acquired several diverse businesses, including Midas Muffler in the automotive industry; a company that made moving walkways for airport terminals; and the largest independent Pepsi bottler in the country.

I was on the ICI board to represent the railroad, but I believed I could contribute sound judgment to all board decisions. At one meeting, Bill Johnson proposed that IC Industries acquire a company called Perfect Plus Hosiery for $9 million. Perfect Plus Hosiery sold stockings on revolving kiosks in grocery stores. Bill believed we could realize significant cost savings from the efficiency of having our Pepsi truck drivers service the panty-hose kiosks while they were restocking the soda shelves.

I imagined burly truck drivers loaded down with heavy cases of drinks while stocking panty hose—and let out a big laugh. Contrary to my notion, the motion to purchase Perfect Plus passed. I abstained from voting. After the meeting Bill called me into his office.

"There's one thing you should understand, Alan. You're on the board because you're president of the railroad. We don't need your views on anything beyond your purview."

I refrained from making any further comments. I took some satisfaction a year later, however, when Bill asked the board's permission to sell Perfect Plus Hosiery at a $3 million loss. The business had been losing a lot of money. My assumption remained that the Pepsi drivers and panty hose weren't a good match. I was quiet as the board approved the sale.

My efforts to lead the railroad into innovation and profit continued to be largely blocked. I never made headway with Gerald Stuckey or the union leaders in Cleveland. And ICC regulations and my fellow railroad presidents hindered needed, meaningful change in the industry.

I felt trapped. It seemed like I was in a room with every door locked. I became disheartened and considered quitting. I had never felt so thoroughly defeated by anything in my life. I more or less gave up and accepted the status quo. I essentially resigned the job.

In the summer of 1976, I was in Pennsylvania playing golf with one of our customers, a steel company executive. Our game was interrupted when I received a call from a friend on the IC Industries board. He told me that my termination was an item on the agenda for the board meeting the following day. I excused myself from the golf game and hurried back to Chicago.

I was at the board meeting when at one point I was asked to leave the room. When I was invited back, the discussion was over and the meeting adjourned.

After the meeting, Bill invited me back to his hotel room and informed me that I was no longer president of the railroad. I would have a new title, vice chairman, and would have my same office, secretary, and salary until the end of the year. I was also given several thousand shares of IC Industries stock options. It was a polite way of saying, "Look for a new job; you're not wanted here."

Bill never responded to my question about why I was being let go. I wondered if my laughter about Perfect Plus Hosiery was a factor in my termination. In fact, during my time with IC, his only response to my annual requests for feedback on performance had been, "You're doing all right." In retrospect, I think the action was appropriate. I should have resigned when I became despondent and accepted the status quo.

After being "fired," I continued going to my office, focusing mostly on looking for a new job. I contacted railroad presidents and friends in the industry. But I found nothing. I considered working for a college or university. I was on Northwestern University's advisory committees for the business school and the transportation center. I had previously been asked if I would be interested in becoming dean of the business school. Because I had just started with the IC, the timing wasn't right. Now I reconsidered a position in academia.

I was invited to Washington University in Saint Louis and UCLA in Los Angeles as a candidate for dean of their respective business schools. I became aware, however, that the role of dean was largely a fund-raising function. I'd never had a problem asking for money, but I decided I did not want to make a career of it.

I was offered a job as vice president of one of the country's largest household moving companies, but that held absolutely no appeal for me. Several Washington law firms pursued me. They wanted me as a "business-getter" for lobbying purposes. Although I think lobbying is an essential part of the legislative process, I had no interest in making it central to my life.

I was fifty-four years old and free of debt. Flavil and I had saved and invested over the years, so we had no financial pressure facing us. Additionally, I earned stipends for serving on the boards of three corporations: Parke-Davis, a pharmacy company;

SCA Services, a large garbage company in Boston; and the Budd Company, which manufactured railroad cars. As the year came to a close and my role as vice chairman ended, I decided to relax and wait to see what would come my way next.

XVI

A Matter of Trust

In February 1977, several months after my tenure at the railroad came to an end, my friend Cyrus Vance called. I had known Cyrus when he was President Johnson's deputy secretary of defense. President Carter had recently appointed him as secretary of state. Cy called to say that he wanted to talk to me about the Bermuda Agreement negotiations.

The Bermuda Agreement, the grandfather of modern international air agreements, had been signed in 1946 between the United States and Britain. But in July 1976, the British government had unilaterally renounced it. Under the terms of the agreement, the countries had one year to negotiate a new one. Failure to reach a new accord by July 1977 meant US and British airlines could no longer fly between the two countries.

Negotiations had begun in 1976, but Cy told me the leaders of the two teams had grown to cordially detest each other. After eight months, the talks were at an impasse. President Carter and Prime Minister Harold Wilson decided to replace the leaders. Cy asked me to assume leadership of the American delegation with the rank of ambassador. I had an excellent background for the operation. I had engaged in similar negotiations while at the Civil

Aeronautics Board, and had experience dealing with international relationships as secretary of transportation. I was also an Anglophile, having developed enormous respect for the English in my posting in England during WWII. I readily accepted.

I spent three weeks at the State Department researching all the files to get up to date on the pertinent issues. President Carter invited me to the White House. He was very welcoming. He thanked me for taking the position. We spoke at length about the negotiations. I was astounded at the depth of his knowledge on the issues. For a man with no background in this area, he had studied enough to be conversant on matters of great detail. He wished me well and told me to keep him informed.

Our delegation was made up of representatives from the State Department, the CAB, and the Commerce Department. We met with the British for a week at a time, alternating between London and Washington, with a few weeks off in between each session.

I found that the US and British positions were basically the same as they had been when I was in London in the 1960s negotiating agreements for the CAB. The United States wanted "open skies" so carriers from either country could have as many flights to as many places as they wished. The British still wanted a 50-50 division of revenue, regardless of which airlines carried the passengers. British airlines were government owned and highly inefficient financially. They did not want to compete with the more efficient, privately owned US airlines. In fact, a British aviation official once told me that BWIA (British West Indian Airways) stood for Britain's Worst Investment Abroad.

My British counterpart was Patrick Shovelton, a senior civil servant in the Ministry of Aviation. Patrick had a good laugh, a big smile, and as strong a desire to reach an agreement as I did. Neither of us wanted to see the end of air service between our two countries. Our meetings were civil and professional. Most of us developed a sincere liking for those we negotiated with on the other side.

Our sessions contained few tense moments and very little anger. On one occasion in London, however, our delegation worked hard to achieve a point we wanted very much, and were successful late one afternoon. But that evening I received a call from Patrick saying that he could not maintain the commitment. Obviously he had been overruled. I was exceedingly angry. If the British made a commitment they could not stick with, there was no reason to think we could trust anything they said. I saw no reason to continue negotiations. Angry as I was, I prepared to depart for home.

Fortunately, before anger became action, cooler heads prevailed. I was instructed that I had to accede to the British retreat on the issue, as our embassy impressed upon me the president's desire to see negotiations continue. That evening, at the home of one of the senior embassy officials, I met for drinks with both Patrick and the UK minister of aviation. I expressed my concern and unhappiness. They listened. And we agreed to move past the discord and continue.

We were in London on the final day of negotiations. By lunch, there was a long list of unresolved issues, some major and some minor. I told my staff to take a break and rest, because we were in for a long night. Negotiations reconvened late in the day. Patrick and I divided our people into groups and assigned each a list of issues to conclude.

Patrick and I wandered separately from group to group to observe progress and to identify areas needing help. About 3:00 a.m., I observed a group led by a young man from my team, Paul Mickey. He was efficiently and methodically completing the items on his list, usually in our favor. I could tell he was very talented. I decided to keep an eye on him for the future.

By six in the morning we had completed every item. The United States certainly did not achieved its main goal of "open skies," nor were we able to accomplish what we hoped for in opening up access for charter airlines. We did, however, achieve an agreement that was reasonable under the circumstances and allowed our airlines to continue to prosper. Clearly the British didn't get everything they wanted either. One major concession we made was a restricted role for charter airlines, which the British thought were unfair competition. To be expected, the agreement was met by grumbling from the US airlines, and by great anger from the charter airlines that thought they were being ignored—although that was clearly not the case. In July we met in Bermuda to sign the final version of the Bermuda Agreement II. With it, we succeeded in averting the cessation of air travel between our countries. President Carter called me three times during the negotiations, but never complained about the results we reached. The "open skies" agreement remained an intractable barrier. I should note that resolution of that issue was not reached for another thirty years.

Flavil and I spent most of the rest of that summer and much of the next year at our vacation home on Lake Delavan, in Wisconsin. It was a two-hour drive from our home in Chicago. Turning into its driveway, you entered a forest and then shortly emerged a few hundred feet farther on into the quiet elegance of the previous century. A large, old house looked down across a well-maintained lawn to the lake. Gaslights illuminated a walkway that circled the shore. On our dock, my fourteen-foot Sunfish sailboat waited to take me out on the water. A small Victorian summer cottage, closer to the lake than the main house, looked like a stage prop for the *Music Man*. In the winter we would cross country ski on the frozen lake.

We had discovered Delavan Lake when we spent several weekends there at the home of Edwin and Martha Vanderwicken. Martha was the one who got me involved in historic preservation. Active in the community, she had been president of the Chicago YWCA, the Cook County School of Nursing, and the Chicago School of Architecture Foundation. She was also part of a group trying to stop the demolition of the last house in Chicago designed by Henry Hobson Richardson, a prominent nineteenth-century architect who had been an important predecessor of Frank Lloyd Wright. However, no one in Martha's group had a connection with Mayor Richard Daley, who always had the final word on all things in Chicago. She asked me to talk to the mayor. And I did. As a result, he agreed to the preservation of the house. It stills stands, designated now as the fascinating Glessner House Museum.

The following year, Martha asked me to join the board of the National Trust for Historic Preservation. Several things about being on the board of the trust appealed to me. I would have the opportunity to travel to its headquarters in Washington, where I still had many friends. The trust's mission of assuming ownership of historic places for preservation fit with my love of history. And I had also been long moved by a comment my friend John Gardner had once made, observing that our structures are the "nonverbal history of America."

I had been on the board for two years when the chairman told me he was resigning for health reasons. Both he and the board wanted me to succeed him, and I was elected chairman. I decided to see if I could make the trust function more efficiently. I engaged the help of one of the other board members, Lawson Knott, whom I had known slightly when he had been President

Johnson's General Services administrator. Lawson and I dug into the workings of the trust. We identified four basic areas that needed action.

First was a $2 million bank loan that had been secured for an unsuccessful membership drive. Second was the trust's willingness to accept any property of historic value without regard to the costs to restore and maintain it. Third, the trust's administrative costs were exceeding its income. And fourth, we believed that Jimmy Biddle needed to be replaced as the trust's president.

Jimmy had a passion for historic preservation and had done good work with the trust for a long time. Our perception, however, was that he wasn't the kind of hard-charging president the trust needed now. Jimmy was functioning more as a figurehead than an executive. I had some history with him from when I was president of the IC. Jimmy had wanted to meet me to solicit a donation. I had been curious about the trust and agreed. He had come to my office, talked for an hour about the trust, then left without asking for a dime. I'd thought, "If his job is to ask for money, he's not very good at it." Lawson and I agreed that a new president was needed.

The board at the time was packed with "do-gooder" conservationists—not pragmatists. Lawson and I convinced them that the trust had to operate more sensibly. They agreed to appoint a new president. One of the first things the new president did was conduct a membership campaign that was so successful, we were able to pay off the $2 million bank loan and cover our administrative costs. The board also decided that going forward, the trust would accept a property only if it came with self-sustaining financial support.

During this time, a staff member of the trust, Mary Means, came up with a crazy but brilliant idea. Instead of focusing only on old historic buildings, Mary thought the trust should expand its mission to preserving historic communities. Older downtown areas were full of history and character, yet many were in stages of advanced decay. She proposed a revitalization program to help communities attract business, customers, and even tourists back to their historic centers. In 1980, the Main Street Four Point Approach, led by Mary, was launched with the support of a sizable grant from a paint company. Since then, the program has helped thousands of communities restore luster to their centers of life and business.

My tenure at the trust ended in 1986, when I reached the nine-year term limit for board membership. I remain, however, proud of the work the trust continues to do, preserving and maintaining significant aspects of our nonverbal history.

XVII

Amtrak

For nearly a full year after the conclusion of the Bermuda Agreement, Flavil and I enjoyed time at the lake while I also attended my board of directors meetings. Life was comfortable, yet I was eager for a new challenge.

In August 1978, I received two phone calls. One was from my friend Don Jacobs, dean of the School of Management at Northwestern University, and one was from Brock Adams, the secretary of transportation in the Carter administration.

Since I was on the Northwestern University advisory board, I knew Don well. Don was also chairman of the board of Amtrak, the National Railroad Passenger Corporation. Don told me that Paul Reistrup, who had worked for me at the Illinois Central, had been fired as Amtrak's president. Don wanted me to replace him.

Brock Adams and I had known each other for many years, since he was a congressman during the time I had been in Washington. Brock also asked me to take over Amtrak. Both Don and Brock told me that Amtrak was in terrible shape, that it needed to be "pulled out of the ditch." They seemed to think that with my excellent relationship with Congress and my railroad leadership experience, I was the one who could save passenger rail service in the United States.

Not wanting to repeat the mistake I'd made when accepting the Illinois Central position, I did research on Amtrak. I knew passenger rail service on the Illinois Central had been a money-losing proposition, as it was for nearly every railroad in the country. Railroads would have long since dropped passenger service entirely if not for the requirements imposed on them by either state authorities or the ICC to maintain certain routes. With no profits from the service to motivate the railroads, most passenger service was horrible, with infrequent departures and dismal on-time performance. Further, they were burdened with old, worn-out cars. Given the state of things, passenger service would have ended if not for the Rail Passenger Service Act of 1970 that President Nixon had signed into law.

The act saved rail passenger service by creating Amtrak as an alternative to nationalizing the passenger rail system, which of course would have been anathema to most Americans. Amtrak was essentially owned by the US government through the Department of Transportation, with the charter to make it a quasi-self-sustaining operation.

When Amtrak started in 1971, two-thirds of all passenger trains that had operated at the end of WWII had been discontinued. What remained of the system was outdated and run-down, including train stations that were crumbling in decay. Unfortunately, that was what Amtrak had been given to start with. In addition, it was given complete ownership of the Northeast Corridor and all of its rolling stock, rails, signal systems, yards, and stations.

Elsewhere in the country, it had to contract with the freight lines. Most railroads viewed passenger trains as a nuisance, and as a result, they would frequently put the Amtrak trains on sidings, giving priority to freight trains. This caused Amtrak schedules to be little more than wishful thinking.

Even fully aware of these obstacles, I decided to take the job. I saw it as an opportunity to serve the public good by working to reinvigorate a worthwhile service. I started with Amtrak at the end of 1978.

My objectives for turning Amtrak around were, first, to review and improve the management team. The second objective was to create a customer-focused operation. Third, I sought to improve relationships with the railroads that were actually carrying all of our long-distance trains. Fourth, I wanted to secure continuing funding for new and reconditioned equipment to improve the quality of our operation. And last, it was imperative that I improve relations with Congress.

At Illinois Central, I had made the mistake of leaving people in jobs who didn't deserve to be there. At Amtrak I wanted a management team that shared my vision, optimism, and energy. I remembered the excitement created by my Department of Transportation leadership group, and I wanted that level of commitment at Amtrak. Changes clearly needed to be made. The first to go was the general counsel, a good lawyer and an old friend of mine, but someone who I thought had retired on the job. I replaced him with Paul Mickey, the young standout from the Bermuda negotiations. Paul was on a fast track to become a partner with one of the best law firms in Washington, so I was delighted when he agreed to leave them and join Amtrak. He proved to be an enormously valuable asset, as well as becoming a close friend.

I enlisted the help of a young executive recruiter, Gary Krauthamer, to head up my search for talent. Gary probed me thoroughly and carefully to make sure that both he and I had a clear understanding of the positions I wanted filled and the work that needed to be accomplished in each position. He was excellent in getting me to think through what it was that I wanted in an effective management team.

My next greatest need was a new vice president of operations. We were fortunate to find him already on staff at Amtrak. He proved to be very competent. We also needed a new chief mechanical officer to deal with our aging rolling stock. Gary hit a home run with Tom Hackney. Tom had been chief mechanical officer of the Chesapeake and Ohio Railroad (C&O), but had reached the C&O mandatory retirement age—a stroke of good luck for us. Tom knew and worked well with all the chief mechanical officers at the freight railroads we dealt with. He was a tremendous help in achieving the objective of improving those relationships. It was quite a bonus that he was also a wonderful human being and a delight to work with.

When Amtrak was given ownership of the Northeast Corridor, it gained not only tracks, stations, rail yards, and old train cars, but also real estate that could be leased or sold for commercial purposes. The real estate was placed under the Sales and Marketing Department, which needed a new vice president. Gary found a gem in Bill Norman, who had been a regional vice president for the Cummins Engine Company.

Clark Tyler, who had worked at the Department of Transportation with me, joined us to take charge of communications, public relations, passenger service, and congressional relationships. In addition to being one of the most decent human beings I've known, he was extremely witty. Clark helped achieve my objective to get all of Amtrak employees to understand and appreciate that the passengers were doing us a favor by riding Amtrak. I wanted all the staff to do everything in their power to keep our passengers happy and to give them a great experience—from getting reservations to buying tickets and riding the trains. During my tenure, Amtrak became exemplary in doing that.

In 1973, the oil consortium, OPEC, imposed an oil embargo. As a consequence, more people started riding trains. Congress decided to allocate funds for Amtrak to purchase its first new cars, dubbed the Amfleet, for short routes. It later allocated funds for the Superliner fleet of double-decker cars for long-distance routes. These Superliner cars were just coming on line when I arrived. About 51 of the planned 284 cars were delivered by the Pullman Company. But we desperately needed improvement with deliveries. None of the cars arrived when promised, and many were four to six months late. Worse, we found that every car they delivered had extensive deficiencies in final assembly. As a result, it took our mechanics much more time to prepare the cars for service than we had anticipated.

A friend of mine who had worked for the Pullman Company suggested I visit the Pullman factory, twenty miles south of Chicago. What I saw appalled me. Brand new seats were stored in puddles of water while they awaited installation. Workers wandered around in slow motion like they were window-shopping. I went to see the CEO, Jim McDivitt, and suggested he visit the plant to see firsthand the problems he had there. He did, but unfortunately not much changed. In spite of the delays, extra repairs, and price overruns, the Superliner cars were ultimately a wise and very successful investment.

Larry Gilson, vice president of government affairs, and Tim Gardner, initially Larry's deputy and later VP of planning and corporate development—both new Amtrak employees—noticed that Congress had inadvertently provided us with an opportunity for an unexpected windfall. It passed a law allowing railroads to sell the tax credits for their depreciable assets, including their rolling stock.

The law was not originally intended to include Amtrak, but Larry discovered that the regulations were written in such a way that they did actually apply to us. I informed Congress that we would be selling some of our tax credits. There were a few grumblings, but because it was within the law, no real opposition materialized. This sale raised enough money to fund another 150 new cars, known as Amfleet II.

Improving relations with Congress was an important part of my job. Amtrak received hundreds of millions of dollars in subsidies each year. I worked to impress upon Congress the importance of passenger rail service and all the good that Amtrak was doing—in spite of the odds. During my initial testimony before the Senate Interstate and Foreign Commerce Committee, a senator criticized Amtrak's expenses and poor on-time record. I pointed out that Amtrak could not provide the fast, safe, reliable service mandated by Congress in 1970 with locomotives built in the 1930s, passenger cars built in the 1940s and '50s, and tracks that had been neglected for years. (In fact, when I told my friend Senator Russell Long of Louisiana that I was returning to Washington to take over Amtrak, he said, "Alan, you have just gotten yourself a rusty old turkey!")

Clark Tyler was a great help when it came to cultivating support in Congress. I would occasionally travel on weekends with members of Congress to their home districts to represent Amtrak. One weekend, I went to Minnesota with Senator Dave Durenberger. Clark arranged a fun event.

The press and the public came to the Minneapolis train station to see the spectacle of Senator Durenberger, whose father had been a locomotive engineer, and the president of Amtrak in a handcar race. The senator and I lined up side by side on separate tracks. When the gun fired, I starting pumping as hard as I could. We stayed even for quite a ways, and then I fell slightly behind. Clark had urged me to let the senator win and look good for his home crowd. I'm confident Dave beat me fair and square.

In 1981, Amtrak encountered another crisis. President Ronald Reagan came into office with a promise to reduce government spending. One of his first proposals was to cut Amtrak funding. I had difficulty understanding the president's reasoning. Amtrak was making excellent progress. I had just reported the results for fiscal year 1980, during which we had 50 percent fewer customer complaints, a 20 percent improvement in on-time performance, a 16 percent revenue growth, and a 4 percent increase in passenger miles—all achieved in spite of an economic recession. When we asked for $970 million for fiscal year 1982, the Reagan administration countered with $613 million.

I went on a publicity offensive, talking to newspapers and anyone else who would listen. I testified before congressional committees and spoke to advocacy groups, spelling out the consequences of the Reagan administration proposal. It would mean ending service in thirty-six states and cause 14,500 employees to lose their jobs. I talked about our renovated equipment, our improved stations, and the new equipment already on order. I said we were about to succeed in carrying out the congressional mandate to establish a sound passenger rail system, and that it made no financial sense to destroy the business when we were making such great strides forward.

It was also imperative that I educate Congress about the reality of funding a rail system. One of my predecessors at

Amtrak had made the unfortunate statement that Amtrak could become financially self-sufficient. That was inaccurate; in fact no passenger rail system in any modern industrial country was completely financially self-sufficient. Fortunately we had some staunch supporters in Congress, as well as a host of supporters in the National Association of Railroad Passengers who were effective in representing the needs of rail passengers to Congress.

The fact remained that the White House budget official I had to deal with held the opinion that the federal government should exist only to fund national defense. Anything else, in his opinion, was a waste. It was a tough negotiation. We got the administration to agree to a budget of $735 million—better than $613 million, but a far cry from what was needed. We were forced to cut routes, including Washington to Cincinnati, Chicago to Duluth, and Seattle to Vancouver, BC. We also had to lay off employees. Fresh meals were replaced with microwaved food.

I came away from the ordeal feeling that Amtrak faced a level of scrutiny seldom imposed on American companies, in spite of our mounting achievements. It was crucial that Amtrak have consistent funding. Toward that end, I created another department, whose mission it was to soften the ongoing budget battles through grants, subsidies, asset utilization, and diversification projects. Larry Gilson took on the additional challenge of creating and leading the new Corporate Development Department. Over the succeeding years, leveraging Amtrak's specialized expertise, underutilized assets, and unique legal status, we were able to enter a range of businesses that proved quite profitable. This effectively helped reduce Amtrak's dependence on congressional appropriations and passenger revenues.

One turn of events that coincidentally helped Amtrak survive when the Reagan administration cut funding was a $45 million lawsuit it won against the Pennsylvania Railroad, about the time I took over at Amtrak. Presciently, I told the vice president of finance to "hide the money." I didn't want to know where, but I knew we're going to need it someday. And we did!

Increasing ridership often overwhelmed the old reservation and ticketing system, causing delays and shutdowns. In 1981, to improve service and increase efficiency, we decided to update it. We hired a contractor to design and install a new electronic reservation system at our national reservation center near Philadelphia. The contractor went to great lengths to assure us that all existing reservations in the system would be carefully backed up and saved in case of a problem with the new system. When they threw the switch and the new system went live, however, every reservation in the entire system disappeared. Completely! We suddenly were faced with running trains with no record of who had tickets, seats, or compartments. It was—to say the least—a disaster.

The staff at the reservation center in Philadelphia set up cots in the offices and halls, and worked day and night to respond to the crisis. Ultimately, they made it work. And the new system did indeed prove to be an improvement. However, without the dedication and hard work of the wonderful people in the reservation center, getting the new system on track would never have happened.

By the spring of 1982, things were operating quite well. The management team was excellent, and we had a good group of employees with a positive attitude about Amtrak. With everyone working together, we had succeeded in managing to pull Amtrak out of the ditch. As a result, it was now on track toward becoming a successful service and important component of the nation's transportation system.

I was deeply pleased with the progress we'd made to date. Amtrak's rolling stock was much improved, we were adding new equipment all the time, and passenger miles continued to climb. Consequently, I was ready to set my sights on new challenges.

There had been interest in the development of high-speed rail service in the United States since the successful inauguration of the Shinkansen, the Japanese high-speed train, and then later the French TGV. Both operated at speeds ranging between 150 and 180 miles per hour. These developments clearly presented an exciting new prospect of service in the United States.

The Japanese National Railroads (JNR) graciously offered to provide a full-time liaison, Gordon Togasaki, as the JNR representative to Amtrak. With his help we developed a relationship with JNR that enabled us to learn from its operations. I went to Tokyo and met Fumio Takagi, the president of the JNR, and we formed a warm relationship that prospered over many years. As a result of our discussions, several of us believed that there was, indeed, a place for a high-speed train in the United States.

Jerry Brown, then governor of California, and his secretary of transportation had been active in improving local commuter trains. With their help, we envisioned building a successful high-speed train between Los Angeles and San Diego. The service would originate at the Los Angeles airport, stop in downtown LA, then make several stops on the way down to San Diego.

I took the idea of operating the high-speed service to the Amtrak board of directors. They, however, had absolutely no interest in the concept. The same was true when I mentioned the idea to members of Congress. Not willing to give up on the idea, I sought a legal opinion to determine if there would be any conflict of interest if I continued as chief executive of Amtrak while also undertaking the promotion of a privately owned, high-speed rail system. It was decided that no conflict existed. That opened the door for us.

Larry Gilson, the driving force behind our efforts to get into high-speed rail, resigned from Amtrak to become president and CEO of the American High Speed Rail Corporation (AHSRC), the enterprise we chartered. Larry had earlier developed relationships with executives at JNR and Kawasaki Heavy Industries, among other Japanese companies, when I had asked him to prepare a backup plan in case the Pullman Company was unable to deliver the Superliner cars Amtrak had on order. The AHSRC board of directors consisted of Larry; myself; Bill MacMillian, a financial adviser with broad ties in international finance; Dick Duchossois, a manufacturer of rail freight cars and the owner of the Arlington Park racetrack in Chicago; and Bill Quinn, the former president of the Burlington Northern Railroad.

The board was an excellent working group. We agreed from the start that we would stay in business only as long as we had enough money to pay the bills—and that we would stop operations before going into debt, regardless of our hopes for the future. That set the stage for us to begin our efforts in obtaining financing.

Larry, along with Gordon Togasaki, helped generate Japanese financial support. We received a loan from the Sumitomo Bank, undoubtedly because of the good offices of Mr. Takagi at JNR. Mr. Ryoichi Sasakawa, a wealthy industrialist with connections to our other supporters in Japan, also contributed a substantial investment. The goal for what we deemed our venture capital "war chest" was reached by a large investment from Dick Duchossois.

With these resources in hand, and benefiting from our relationships with Governor Brown, the Japanese National Railroads, and others, we began to make substantial progress. We obtained the rights to a continuous right-of-way from San Diego to downtown Los Angeles, and then on to the Los Angeles airport. A team from JNR that had built the high-speed Shinkansen came to Los Angeles, and working with Fluor Daniel, our US engineering firm, we completed the preliminary system design and prepared the construction cost estimate. In addition, we prepared and filed a complete environmental impact assessment. Three of the largest US construction companies formed a partnership to build the project.

Arthur D. Little, our consultant, completed a passenger revenue forecast. It projected that there would be enough passenger traffic to generate sufficient income to meet both our operating and our investment costs. The California legislature passed special legislation allowing American High Speed Rail to issue tax-exempt bonds to fund a portion of the construction.

The First Boston Company was retained to secure funding for the project. They were supportive of our efforts to arrange a lending syndicate composed of Japanese and American banks, although Larry Gilson, Bill MacMillan, and I did most of the work. Before we could proceed to issuing the tax-exempt bonds, we needed to complete an initial round of equity funding. First Boston insisted that we commission additional studies to replicate those done by Arthur D. Little, the JNR, and the Fluor Daniel experts. First Boston also specified the consultants to perform these studies, which required doubling the initial equity investment from $30 million to $60 million. It then pledged to take the lead in raising the additional funds.

Our board worked hard and arranged commitments for half the required total. Unfortunately, First Boston never raised any money. We were subsequently unable to raise the balance, and thus could not proceed with the bond issue.

Failure to procure financing dealt a fatal blow to the project. The increased equity investment above the $30 million we were able to raise was too big of a hurdle. Out of money and out of possibilities, with our remaining venture capital funding just sufficient to provide a modest severance to our employees and pay our vendors, we closed the operation with sadness.

This was extremely hard to accept, especially since our conservative cost and revenue projections indicated the project was viable, that it would be able to pay its operating expenses from the first day of service and soon begin to pay off the bonds. If we'd been successful, passengers would have traveled between LA and San Diego in less than an hour at speeds up to 160 miles per hour. The end of the American High Speed Rail Corporation was a great loss for rail travel in the United States.

The dream had not died for me, however. I subsequently got involved in another attempt to establish a high-speed rail link. My friend Jeeb Halaby asked me to join the board of a company proposing to build a high-speed train between Washington, DC, and Dulles Airport. We gained the support of many businesses in the area.

The local county transit planners, however, opposed it. Though the Metro trains from downtown Washington stopped twelve miles short of the airport, they insisted that bus service was adequate to meet travelers' needs. They refused to believe projections for tremendous future growth in passenger volume at Dulles, which would clearly exceed the capacity of a bus system. We argued strenuously that air travelers expected both the speed and convenience of a direct link to Washington. The local county "experts" would not budge. Their resistance killed the project.

This effectively ended my high-speed train career. It also ended the best opportunity for Americans to discover how pleasant, efficient, and fast traveling by train can be.

I left Amtrak the last day of May 1982 to become CEO of Airbus Industrie of North America. I took with me a sense of accomplishment at Amtrak, leaving behind an improved organization—from its management team and staff, down to the track and rolling stock on the ground. Despite numerous hurdles we faced, we had done it through creative ingenuity and teamwork.

Possibly the best thing I accomplished for Amtrak was to talk my friend Graham Claytor into replacing me as president. Graham, a lawyer, had been acting secretary of the Department of Transportation, and was formerly secretary of the navy and president of the Southern Railroad. He was an excellent railroad man and a train enthusiast as well—including having a model train system at his house that was big enough to sit on and ride around the yard. With the hiring of Graham as CEO, my final goal to upgrade the quality of top leadership at Amtrak was achieved.

XVIII

Airbus

In March 1982, two months before I left Amtrak, Don Agger called me. Don had been my assistant secretary for international aviation at the Department of Transportation. He called to say that Airbus Industrie was looking for a new chief executive officer for their North American subsidiary, Airbus Industrie of North America. And that he had recommended me as the person Airbus Industrie needed. He believed—correctly so—that I would be able to contact the chief executives of the airlines and get an audience for Airbus that they, as yet, had been unable to attain.

Airbus was a consortium of European aerospace companies. It built a twin-engine, 300-plus-seat commercial passenger plane that competed against Boeing and McDonnell Douglas, the dominant producers of commercial aircraft in the world. The A300 had not been able to gain success in the North American market, except for the lease of planes to Eastern Airlines when they were financially unable to purchase Boeing aircraft. Only eighty-one A300s had been delivered worldwide by 1980, so US airlines were understandably cautious about adopting them.

The idea of going to work for Airbus was intriguing. I flew to Toulouse and met Bernard Lathiere, the chief executive, and

Roger Beteille, the executive vice president of Airbus Industrie. We went to a quiet villa for lunch, where we conversed about the American market, the European market, the concept of Airbus, and their hopes.

Bernard was a genius. I believe he graduated from college at seventeen, and was immediately named an inspector of finance, a post that the French civil service used as a means of designating those people whom it expected to be future government leaders. Roger was equally brilliant. An aircraft engineer, he was the technical father of Airbus. He outlined the structure of what parts of an Airbus plane would be constructed by which countries. Both men spoke excellent English and asked very pointed questions. They also gave comprehensive answers to my equally direct questions. I was impressed. They were extremely knowledgeable in their roles, and I enjoyed their humor. By the end of lunch I liked them both.

I toured the assembly line, viewing planes at various stages of production. Even as a layman, I was satisfied that the planes were made with fine materials and excellent craftsmanship. I felt I would have no problem endorsing or promoting them. I also met several Airbus vice presidents, all of whom I liked.

Before leaving Toulouse, I met again with Bernard and Roger. They told me they would like to have me join them. I said I would, if they agreed to certain conditions. My first condition was that I report directly to Bernard, the CEO, not to the senior vice president of marketing, as earlier chief executives of Airbus North America had. They readily assented.

My second condition was that I would not move to New York City, where the Airbus North American headquarters were, but would continue to live in Washington. I told them I would commute to New York during the week and spend as much time there as necessary, but that I would retain my residence in Washington.

My third condition was that I be permitted to continue my work with the American High Speed Rail Corporation, which at the time had not yet run into difficulty. They agreed to all my conditions.

On June 1, 1982, I traveled to the office of Airbus Industrie of North America in Rockefeller Center in Manhattan. The original Airbus people in Toulouse had made Manhattan the headquarters for the US subsidiary because New York was the financial center of the United States, and they assumed that all important businesses were there.

The office was small. It consisted of a receptionist/secretary, a bookkeeper, three so-called salesmen, and myself. It functioned as a combination public relations and marketing operation. The salesmen did not, in fact, do any selling or make any proposals. They provided the airlines with information on the Airbus equipment, such as range, capacity, comfort, and reliability; and provided comparisons with the various competitive aircraft in the Boeing and McDonnell Douglas families.

Selling was done only by people from Toulouse. The North American subsidiary did nothing but stand by and provide assistance to the negotiators. The New York office was responsible, however, for preparing advertising campaigns that were put into aviation publications and for sending staff to various aviation industry events to distribute brochures. It also gave members of Congress and the administration information about Airbus Industrie.

I rented a small, two-bedroom suite in Le Parker Meridian hotel, overlooking Central Park, only five blocks from my office. My routine was to arrive in New York City on Tuesday morning and return to Washington Thursday evening.

I arranged to visit every airline CEO to talk about the benefits of Airbus without denigrating the other manufacturers. Although the CEOs, without exception, were friendly and courteous, I faced a decidedly uphill battle. They listened as I explained that Airbus planes, then the A300 and the new A310, offered several advantages. They were wider, allowing either wider aisles or a few more inches per seat. They were quieter, and they also had a standardized cockpit design, a wonderful innovation. Our competitors' planes had different cockpit configurations for each of their models, requiring additional training for pilots and mechanics.

I also believed Airbus planes were built with greater precision. I didn't have scientific proof, but that belief was grounded in my first tour of the Toulouse factory. Felix Kracht, a German engineer, gave me the tour of the final assembly line that he both designed and supervised. An excellent pilot, he was famous for being the first man to fly over the Alps in a glider he had designed and built, a feat he was rightfully proud of. I think Felix was more proud of the precision and efficiency of his assembly line than he was of his personal achievements. I asked him what happened if a part arrived from a supplier that didn't fit his tolerances.

"We say to them, 'You come and get your damn junk right now!'" he retorted.

Since the A300 was a relatively new airplane, it had not had time to develop the reputation for safety and reliability it eventually achieved. Fewer than a hundred had been in operation around the world since its launch in 1974. In addition, some US airlines had had previous negative experiences with European manufacturers because they hadn't been able to receive replacement parts in a timely manner.

Even though US airlines were open to all possibilities, there was, in fact, a "buy American" attitude. The CEO of United told me outright, "I'm going to buy an American airplane." I pointed out that buying an American airplane actually meant buying a plane with numerous parts made in Japan, Canada, and elsewhere, and that an Airbus airplane included many parts that were made in America. In fact, there wasn't a huge difference. His response was, "I'm going to buy an airplane with an American name on it—regardless of where the parts come from." That ended our conversation. I'm happy to say that after he left the airline, United became one of the largest Airbus customers worldwide.

Unfortunately, my challenges in the early going were further compounded by the fact that I had asked to report directly to the CEO. That change in the reporting structure created an enemy for me. The senior vice president of marketing spent months working to undermine me. He caused me considerable angst during that stage, when I had not yet developed enough friends in Toulouse who could help me understand what was going on. I was relieved when he was fired for reasons that had nothing to do with me.

Another element of my uphill battle was customer loyalty. I met with Don Nyrop, who had been Northwest's CEO since the mid-1950s. Don said that he had no doubt that Airbus made wonderful airplanes, and that in other circumstances he would have been happy to take a serious look. However, "I'm going to buy Boeing aircraft," he said. He told me that when he became president of the airline, it was close to bankruptcy. Jets had just come in. "In 1959 we had no jets and no money to buy jets. I went to see the CEO of Boeing, Bill Allen, and told him my situation. I stated that if I was going to stay in business, I needed jets," Don explained. "Bill just asked me how many I needed. That started us on the road to recovery. I can't turn my back on Boeing, Alan."

"And you shouldn't," I answered, admiring his loyalty.

A major barrier for us in gaining entry to the US market was Boeing's willingness to preserve a sale—preventing one for us— at all costs, regardless of how much money it lost. Boeing was fierce in its determination to prevent Airbus from penetrating the US market, which was where the majority of global new orders for planes were made.

I remember an incident with Piedmont Airlines that clearly illustrated this point. Piedmont was thinking about expanding into London. We knew they were talking to Boeing about buying the Boeing 767 for that route. We put together a proposal for two A310s, which would fit their needs very well. I flew to Greensboro, North Carolina, to talk with Bill Howard, Piedmont's CEO. Bill and I had been friends since my time at the CAB, when he had been a lawyer with Eastern Airlines.

I presented Bill with our proposal. He was interested, but told me Boeing was offering the 767s for a lower price.

"Give me until the morning, Bill, to see what I can do," I said.

All financial decisions ultimately came from Toulouse. I went back to my hotel and called Roger. The executive committee met and approved a figure that I was sure would win the deal. I went to Bill's office the next morning full of confidence, only to discover that Frank Shrontz, the Boeing president, had visited Piedmont the previous evening.

"Alan, Frank offered us two 767s at whatever price we're willing to pay," Bill told me. "I doubt Airbus can beat that."

And he was right. It's ironic that Boeing later accused Airbus of selling planes at a loss to gain market share.

If the barriers weren't high enough already, another hurdle to gaining a foothold with US airlines was Boeing's superb customer service. Its distribution center was in the United States, meaning that Boeing could deliver parts anywhere in the country in a matter of hours. The Airbus service center was in Hamburg, Germany. Airbus promised to supply parts within twenty-four hours, but potential clients wondered how successful we'd actually be at that. Besides, twenty-four hours is an eternity when your plane is sitting on the ground waiting for parts instead of in the air making money.

As we tried to build the North American market, Bernard and Roger would sometimes come to the United States to meet with potential clients and with our suppliers. The two of them together would have been unbeatable, brilliant as they were, but Bernard's love of alcohol was a significant problem.

Bernard and I visited the General Electric jet engine manufacturing plant in Cincinnati. The following day a GE executive took us by private plane to New York to meet with Jack Welch, the CEO of General Electric. I had called ahead to the GE executive who would accompany us on the plane and asked him to remove all alcohol from the jet. He was aware of Bernard's alcohol addiction and knew that I didn't want Bernard arriving drunk for the New York meeting.

I was stunned and angry when he offered Bernard a drink as soon as we were in the air. I have no idea why he intentionally sabotaged our meeting with Jack Welch. Predictably, Bernard was inebriated when we arrived. The meeting with Welch was rather brusque and short—and unproductive.

In 1985, Bernard was replaced by Jean Pierson as CEO of Airbus. Bernard had been charming and politically savvy, whereas Pierson, on the other hand, was plainspoken and direct. He was a no-nonsense engineer's engineer. He would pound his desk to make a point.

I was in Toulouse the day Pierson was inaugurated as chairman. He addressed most of the personnel of the Toulouse operation in a big auditorium. He declared that things were going to change. He was going to personally examine every expense report. "No one is going to wander into work at ten o'clock like they are used to doing," he scolded.

He went on in this vein until a German engineer stood up. "Mr. Pierson, you don't know what you're talking about."

The engineer happened to be right. The work ethic in Toulouse was exemplary. Everyone in the audience, however, myself included, expected that the outspoken engineer would shortly be fired. I was surprised when I returned to Toulouse in a few weeks and heard that Pierson had called that engineer into his office—not to fire him, but to ask for advice.

I was impressed. The action increased my respect for Pierson, knowing he would seek counsel from someone who had publicly challenged him.

Pierson was suspicious by nature, however. I was an unknown quantity to him. Consequently, he sent Michel Grand to New York to keep an eye on things. Michel took over my CEO responsibilities, leaving me as chairman and freeing me from the day-to-day operations. Michel was all right, though we never warmed to each other.

Grand had been in the New York office about a year and a half when I discovered that he was signing my name to documents. The papers were routine matters, like insignificant board actions. But being insignificant didn't make the behavior any more acceptable. I was outraged. I told Pierson that Michel had crossed the line. I couldn't work for a company where someone could sign my name without first gaining my consent. Pierson invited me to come to Toulouse.

Pierson's assistant, a nice young man, met me at the airport in Paris to take me out for coffee.

"Pierson doesn't want you to quit," he told me. "What Grand did was wrong. Pierson knows that. He'll see that it never happens again. Just don't quit."

In Toulouse I met Pierson. He listened as I let off steam about Grand. Pierson was gracious—and agreed with me.

"You've done a good job for Airbus," he told me. "I want you to stay. I don't want to lose you."

We shook hands. And that ended the matter. I felt that it was important to have my say, and I did. I stayed with Airbus, and shortly thereafter, Michel was moved to Toulouse. I doubt the move had as much to do with the "forgeries" as with Pierson being finally convinced that no one in New York was stealing pencils or paper clips.

Dealing with Toulouse was occasionally frustrating. As brilliant as the French are, they sometimes have an unshakeable belief in the correctness of their opinion. I think that may be what led their former president, Charles de Gaulle, to say with frustration and humor, "How can anyone be expected to govern a nation that has 246 kinds of cheese?"

I had a hard time convincing Toulouse of the needs of the American market. They thought they knew more about Americans than I did on at least two issues: one, the need for locating a parts service center in North America; and two, its perception of the size of the United States—and what that required in the design of planes.

Airbus was designing its new A320 series with a maximum range of 1,500 miles. That was more than adequate for the map of Europe, but I kept telling them, "Folks, that's not enough range in the US. Look at the map. It's three thousand miles coast to coast." They didn't think I knew what I was talking about. They refused to believe US airlines wanted a plane with transcontinental range.

They were wrong. The A320 was a success worldwide—except in North America. People in Toulouse realized that my advice was, in fact, solid when Delta Airlines refused to consider buying the A320 unless it had a transcontinental range. The A320's range was quickly increased to cover the entire continent.

With regard to serving its customers, I told Pierson that Airbus would never develop a significant presence in North America until its customer service was on par with Boeing's. This meant establishing a service center in the United States. The timing for considering this was difficult. Airbus was pouring money into developing the A320.

Once again, it was an airline that forced Toulouse to appreciate the wisdom of my advice. Continental Airlines, which had a leased fleet of Airbus planes, got fed up waiting for parts. CEO Frank Lorenzo pointedly told Pierson to come get all of his "#@/*-!! planes." The adjectives were far from complimentary.

Thanks in large part to Continental and the new A320s coming online, Pierson chose to expand operations in North America with both a service center and an increased sales staff. I recommended another change that would benefit both Airbus and myself: moving the North American headquarters from New York to Washington.

Pierson was easily persuaded. I had found a location on the service road to Dulles Airport to house our headquarters at a third of the cost of the New York office. I located property three miles away for the service center. The entire staff, with the exception of one secretary, moved to Washington. I had already replaced two of the salesmen, and after we moved, I asked Gary Krauthamer to help me find and hire five more excellent people. One of them was John Leahy. Tenacious and brilliant, John would not take no for an answer—from any client. John is now in senior management in Toulouse as chief operating officer for customers. He has sold more planes than anyone else in the world.

The new A320s were easier to sell than the A300s or the A310s, both long-range, wide-body planes. The A320s were narrow-bodied, with seating for up to 220 passengers, and good for the more frequent short-to-medium-range routes. The A320s were also the first jets to use a wingtip device for fuel efficiency. In flight, a traditional plane wing creates a vortex at the tip that increases drag. The A320's wingtip "fence," as it was called, turns up at the wingtip to disrupt the vortex. This advance both reduced drag and saved fuel. When the A320 inaugurated the feature, Boeing mocked it as ridiculous. A few years later, however, Boeing launched its own wingtip device.

The A320s and our excellent sales staff finally started making inroads into the US market. Boeing's arrogance certainly helped. Several airlines told us that Boeing behaved as though it knew more about what their airline needed than the airline executives. It seemed like people from Boeing came to sales meetings to tell the airline, "This is what you need. Take it." Our staff on the other hand, worked to understand the needs of the airlines and provide support. Customers came to feel that Airbus was part of their team.

Our first big order came from Northwest Airlines. This was followed by United, then US Airways, America West, and Air Canada. The competition between Airbus and Boeing quickly became fierce on every sale.

Boeing was not happy to see Airbus selling planes in its backyard. It started a political and media crusade against us, accusing Airbus of unfair trade practices, like dumping planes in the North American market. They implied that Airbus was selling planes at a price that was less than the production costs (failing to mention its own gifts of planes at any price made previously to Piedmont Airlines and others).

Boeing also focused on the fact that the Airbus had received $9 billion in government loans and subsidies. It misrepresented the loans as gifts. They tried to pressure the Reagan administration into filing trade complaints against the four consortium countries—France, Britain, Germany, and Spain.

The fact is that Airbus did receive subsidies in the form of no-interest or low-interest loans from the four consortium governments. But the terms of the loans required repayment of the majority of the funds. And Airbus did, in fact, pay back its loans.

At the same time, Boeing received a substantial amount of money, equipment, and engineering expertise through indirect subsidies from the Department of Defense and from the National Aeronautics and Space Administration (NASA). This came in the form of military contracts. Boeing was paid for research and development work, and received free help from NASA and Department of Defense engineers. It also received free use of government testing facilities and equipment. Boeing was allowed to keep all of the production machinery, patents, and intellectual property derived from these military contracts, which was naturally of sizable benefit to its civil aircraft division.

Accusations between Boeing and Airbus escalated throughout the 1980s. When the World Trade Organization investigated the claims, they found that both Boeing and Airbus were right. Both were receiving subsidies. Finally, the two manufacturers started negotiations to avoid a debilitating trade war between the United States and Europe. It took five years to negotiate the US-EU Agreement on Large Civil Aircraft, which was finally signed in 1992.

The agreement restricted direct subsidies to 33 percent of the development cost of new aircraft, along with strengthening rules about interest rates and royalties for paying back the subsidies. The agreement also restricted indirect subsidies to 3 percent of the United States' aerospace industry turnover, a complicated calculation to be performed every year. Boeing, however, was not required to pay back the indirect subsidies.

I believed the direct subsidies to Airbus and the indirect subsidies to Boeing basically leveled the playing field. Unfortunately, however, Boeing's campaign succeeded in tarnishing Airbus's standing with North American buyers.

I tried to persuade Pierson to wean Airbus off subsidies so we would be seen as a free-market competitor. I wrote a long dissertation outlining my thoughts. I may have been the first to make this argument, but I wasn't the last. In the early 1990s Pierson did try to convert Airbus into a conventional corporation. He retired before the convoluted legal issues were finally ironed out. The change was completed in 2001.

When the 1992 US-EU agreement was signed, I was seventy-one. I had been involved in improving transportation for many years. Throughout my career I had noticed a propensity for people to hang on to their jobs too long, well past when they were significantly contributing to an organization. I would think, "Why don't they leave and make room for someone else?" Although, even at seventy-one I was making solid contributions, I didn't have the energy or the creative ingenuity I'd once had. For the first time in my career, I didn't feel a driving need for new challenges. It was time to leave.

EPILOGUE

More than twenty years have passed since I retired. Reflecting on my life, my values, my friendships, and my family are what I prize most.

I've always worked hard and tried to do what is right. That requires an internal compass, a set of values and beliefs, to guide my actions and decisions. The values I used as a guide have served me well. I believe they're worth sharing.

I believe in honesty. Like the University of Virginia, I have an honor code I follow. I know I could not live with myself if I ever lied or cheated. I want to look in the mirror every day and be proud of the person I see.

I believe in fairness, which I learned from my mother. Fairness makes life better for everyone. The definition of fairness I like most is "I'll cut the cake and you can choose which piece is yours."

I believe in equality—again something I learned from my mother. She taught me that we are all children of God without regard to color or circumstance. A statement of this is "I believe I am as good as everyone else, and everyone else is as good as I am."

I believe in helping others. My experience in government affirmed my belief that one essential function of government is to help others. I'm saddened and troubled to see this ideal demonized today. The government in our country really is "of the people, by the people, and for the people." It is tragic that some segments of society seem to forget that.

Personally, I owe much of my good fortune to people who helped me along the way. I know that some people think the way to climb the ladder of success is to approach life as a competition that requires knocking others out of the way as they dash to the top. I prefer to give a hand to people coming up the ladder—and to those about to fall off. In this way we all succeed. I have been rewarded in my life for endeavoring to make people and organizations work well as a whole rather than focusing on my own success alone.

I believe in preparing for what you want. I've been lucky in life, but I wanted and sought challenges—and I was prepared when they appeared.

I believe in saving. Everyone needs money, not simply for retirement, but for personal and family crises—which are never planned. That said, after a certain amount, I've found that how much money I have has little effect on my satisfaction with life. I never pursued money for its own sake, and instead, sought satisfaction in my choices—in friends, in family, and in my career.

I believe in action. When challenged, you can either wait to see what happens or you can act. I've always been in the do-something camp. You may not get the outcome you're hoping for, but if nothing else, you will have gained a fresh perspective.

I believe in self-confidence. I never set out to walk across Niagara Falls on a high wire, but I believed I could do whatever I set my mind to. Confidence is a prerequisite to success. I could not have enjoyed the rich career and life I've had without it.

I believe in optimism. When challenged I'd ask myself, "What can I do to make this better? How can I bring greater joy to myself and others?"

I believe in friendship. Over the years I have been blessed with many friends. I've come to appreciate that the world is full of thoughtful, interesting, kind, and caring people. It has been a great pleasure to get to know so many of them.

I have been immensely fortunate in work, in travel, and in friends—but most importantly in family. Flavil, Mark, his wife, Nancy, and my two wonderful grandchildren, Heather and Alan, have been my greatest fortune of all. They are the true wealth of my life.

Flavil was two months shy of her eighty-ninth birthday when she died. We'd been happily married for more than sixty-four years. Not only did we love each other, but we respected each other—even when hanging wallpaper. We were both quite liberal in our politics, and we shared many of the same beliefs—beliefs based in values that guided us in everything we did.

I have lived ninety-three wonderful years. My life has spanned most of the twentieth century and has carried me well into the start of the twenty-first. I've seen a lot of change, and I've created some of it. Inside, I remain essentially that curious boy who wants to learn new things, wants to make the world better, and looks forward to meeting new friends. I have encountered a few thorns along the way, but mostly, my life has been a bed of roses.

ACKNOWLEDGMENTS

Many people have helped me remember and record my life. I deeply appreciate all of their help. If there are errors in this memoir, I wish to take full credit for them, since I probably wanted life to happen the way I remembered it—whether it was true or not. Each of these wonderful people has helped me refine and improve the recounting of my fortunate experiences.

Maureen Lander helped bring an initial structure to these musings. Sonja Peterson-Lewis, who grew up in Macclenny and knew my sister, Jean, was kind enough to read and comment on my Baker County reflections. Jean's son Mark Dowling and his wife, Ethel, were generous in sharing Jean's collection of pictures from our early years.

Roger Day, author of *Membury at War,* and local history expert, Mick Dowdeswell, took me back to the Membury runway I departed from on D-Day to celebrate the seventieth anniversary of that event. Charlie Walker, whose family now owns the runway, was our gracious host. The wonderful quote about my flying salute to Paris was found by Patricia Overman during her research on troop carrier pilots.

Essential to the creation of the Department of Transportation, Cecil Mackey prodded my memory and reviewed my writing. Jeff Davis, who is researching documents relating to the creation of the DOT, generously shared his discoveries. I hope he writes his own book soon. An expert on transportation statistics, Alan Pisarski, was helpful in keeping my numbers from being too far off the mark. Larry Gilson, my good friend and colleague at Amtrak and American High Speed Rail, provided essential feedback on that period.

Careful reading of the drafts by Mercedes Lawry, Yvonne Hunt, Teresa Sparkman, and Nancy Lomneth have made positive contributions to the clarity of the final product.

Frank O Smith deserves all the credit for guiding me through the process of turning my efforts into a book. Frank's skill with both words and the publishing process have been invaluable.

My son, Mark, is fully to blame for this whole project. He encouraged me to record my memories for my grandchildren, Heather and Alan. Mark provided a digital recorder and transcribed the results onto the written page. He wrote and rewrote multiple drafts, seeking to make it concise while retaining my "voice." At this point he knows more about my life than I do. I can't thank him enough.

Finally, I would like to acknowledge my friend and companion Mimi Pierce, who enriches my life in the present.